D1432762

OPPOSING VIEWPOINTS® SERIES

Sexual Assault on Campus

Other Books of Related Interest:

"Congress shall make
no law ... abridging
the freedom of speech,
or of the press."

First Amendment to the US Constitution

The basic foundation of our democracy is the First Amendment guarantee of freedom of expression. The Opposing Viewpoints series is dedicated to the concept of this basic freedom and the idea that it is more important to practice it than to enshrine it.

OPPOSING
VIEWPOINTS®
SERIES

Sexual Assault on Campus

Jack Lasky, Book Editor

GREENHAVEN PRESS
A part of Gale, Cengage Learning

GALE
CENGAGE Learning·

Farmington Hills, Mich • San Francisco • New York • Waterville, Maine
Meriden, Conn • Mason, Ohio • Chicago

GALE
CENGAGE Learning·

Judy Galens, *Manager, Frontlist Acquisitions*

For more information, contact:
Greenhaven Press
27500 Drake Rd.
Farmington Hills, MI 48331-3535
Or you can visit our Internet site at gale.cengage.com

For product information and technology assistance, contact us at

Gale Customer Support, 1-800-877-4253
For permission to use material from this text or product, submit all requests online at www.cengage.com/permissions

Further permissions questions can be emailed to permissionrequest@cengage.com

Articles in Greenhaven Press anthologies are often edited for length to meet page requirements. In addition, original titles of these works are changed to clearly present the main thesis and to explicitly indicate the author's opinion. Every effort is made to ensure that Greenhaven Press accurately reflects the original intent of the authors. Every effort has been made to trace the owners of copyrighted material.

LIBRARY OF CONGRESS CATALOGING-IN-PUBLICATION DATA

Names: Lasky, Jack, editor.
Title: Sexual assault on campus / Jack Lasky, book editor.
Description: Farmington Hills, Mich : Greenhaven Press, a part of Gale,
  Cengage Learning, [2016] | Series: Opposing viewpoints | Includes
  bibliographical references and index.
Identifiers: LCCN 2015026270 | ISBN 9780737775600 (hardcover) | ISBN
  9780737775617 (pbk.)
Subjects: LCSH: Rape in universities and colleges--United States. | Rape in
  universities and colleges--United States--Prevention. | Women college
  students--Crimes against--United States.
Classification: LCC LB2345.3.R37 S487 2016 | DDC 371.7/82--dc23
LC record available at http://lccn.loc.gov/2015026270

Printed in Mexico
1 2 3 4 5 6 7 19 18 17 16

Contents

Chapter 3: How Might the College Sexual Assault Problem Be Addressed?

Chapter 4: What Other Factors Are Tied to the Campus Sexual Assault Problem?

Why Consider
Opposing Viewpoints?

> *"The only way in which a human being can make some approach to knowing the whole of a subject is by hearing what can be said about it by persons of every variety of opinion and studying all modes in which it can be looked at by every character of mind. No wise man ever acquired his wisdom in any mode but this."*
>
> *John Stuart Mill*

In our media-intensive culture it is not difficult to find differing opinions. Thousands of newspapers and magazines and dozens of radio and television talk shows resound with differing points of view. The difficulty lies in deciding which opinion to agree with and which "experts" seem the most credible. The more inundated we become with differing opinions and claims, the more essential it is to hone critical reading and thinking skills to evaluate these ideas. Opposing Viewpoints books address this problem directly by presenting stimulating debates that can be used to enhance and teach these skills. The varied opinions contained in each book examine many different aspects of a single issue. While examining these conveniently edited opposing views, readers can develop critical thinking skills such as the ability to compare and contrast authors' credibility, facts, argumentation styles, use of persuasive techniques, and other stylistic tools. In short, the Opposing Viewpoints Series is an ideal way to attain the higher-level thinking and reading skills so essential in a culture of diverse and contradictory opinions.

In addition to providing a tool for critical thinking, Opposing Viewpoints books challenge readers to question their own strongly held opinions and assumptions. Most people form their opinions on the basis of upbringing, peer pressure, and personal, cultural, or professional bias. By reading carefully balanced opposing views, readers must directly confront new ideas as well as the opinions of those with whom they disagree. This is not to argue simplistically that everyone who reads opposing views will—or should—change his or her opinion. Instead, the series enhances readers' understanding of their own views by encouraging confrontation with opposing ideas. Careful examination of others' views can lead to the readers' understanding of the logical inconsistencies in their own opinions, perspective on why they hold an opinion, and the consideration of the possibility that their opinion requires further evaluation.

Evaluating Other Opinions

To ensure that this type of examination occurs, Opposing Viewpoints books present all types of opinions. Prominent spokespeople on different sides of each issue as well as well-known professionals from many disciplines challenge the reader. An additional goal of the series is to provide a forum for other, less known, or even unpopular viewpoints. The opinion of an ordinary person who has had to make the decision to cut off life support from a terminally ill relative, for example, may be just as valuable and provide just as much insight as a medical ethicist's professional opinion. The editors have two additional purposes in including these less known views. One, the editors encourage readers to respect others' opinions—even when not enhanced by professional credibility. It is only by reading or listening to and objectively evaluating others' ideas that one can determine whether they are worthy of consideration. Two, the inclusion of such viewpoints encourages the important critical thinking skill of objectively evaluating an author's credentials and bias. This evaluation will illuminate an author's reasons for taking a particular stance on an issue and will aid in readers' evaluation of the author's ideas.

It is our hope that these books will give readers a deeper understanding of the issues debated and an appreciation of the complexity of even seemingly simple issues when good and honest people disagree. This awareness is particularly important in a democratic society such as ours in which people enter into public debate to determine the common good. Those with whom one disagrees should not be regarded as enemies but rather as people whose views deserve careful examination and may shed light on one's own.

Thomas Jefferson once said that "difference of opinion leads to inquiry, and inquiry to truth." Jefferson, a broadly educated man, argued that "if a nation expects to be ignorant and free . . . it expects what never was and never will be." As individuals and as a nation, it is imperative that we consider the opinions of others and examine them with skill and discernment. The Opposing Viewpoints series is intended to help readers achieve this goal.

David L. Bender and Bruno Leone,
Founders

Introduction

> *"Sexual assault, domestic violence, dating violence, and stalking are serious problems on college and university campuses. . . . Nineteen percent of undergraduate women reported experiencing completed or attempted sexual assault since entering college. Most of these assaults were committed by someone the victim knew, and these perpetrators are often serial offenders. Rape frequently devastates the victim and derails her education and her future."*
>
> —*"Responding to Campus Sexual Assault,"*
> United States Department of Justice,
> May 13, 2015

Colleges have long had a reputation for being hotbeds of sexual activity. This fact is hardly surprising, considering that these institutions are populated by an enormous number of young people in their sexual prime who are living away from home for the first time and have easy access to alcohol and drugs. Thanks in part to the sexual revolution of the 1960s, sparked by the advent of the birth control pill, sexual activity has become a normal part of life on college campuses across the United States and a widely accepted cultural norm. Unfortunately, the collegiate sexual culture has a dark side: American colleges now face what activists call an epidemic of sexual assault.

Studies have shown that sexual assaults likely occur on today's college campuses at an alarming rate. While critics frequently dispute the exact figures regarding these incidents, evidence suggests that campus sexual assaults are a legitimate concern, at least to some extent. However, the campus sexual assault problem remains a highly controversial matter that tends to be deeply divisive along gender, political, and other lines. Indeed, the ongoing debate over this issue encompasses not only the alleged seriousness of the problem but also its possible causes, its handling by college officials and outside authorities, how it might be better addressed, and more.

To truly understand the campus sexual assault problem, one must first know exactly what sexual assault is. Today experts typically define sexual assault as the act of forcing someone to engage in any sort of unwanted sexual contact, from nonconsensual kissing to nonconsensual intercourse. Historically, however, such behavior was not always seen as a form of abuse or even aggression. In earlier ages, sexual assault often was viewed as a normal method of seduction. Only when people began to think of the practice as unacceptable did sexual assault become recognized as a deviant and even criminal form of behavior. So, if sexual assault is believed to be wrong, why does it allegedly happen so frequently on college campuses?

Given the controversy surrounding the extent of the campus sexual assault crisis, it is hardly surprising that agreement on the causes of the problem also is lacking. In general, most experts would concur that the age of the students involved, the consumption of alcohol, and the norms of male college sexuality all play some role. Beyond those factors, however, pinpointing a precise explanation for what has led campus sexual assault to become such an apparently rampant issue is difficult. Some place blame on fraternities and their notoriously out-of-control parties. Others argue that administrative failures are to blame. Still others point to the alleged prevalence of "rape culture" in contemporary society. Unfortunately, simple, clear-cut answers do not seem to exist.

The possible causes of the campus sexual assault problem are, however, only one part of the broader conversation on the topic. Many have raised questions about how campus sexual assault accusations should be handled, whether the approaches colleges take in response to such matters are fair to both accusers and the accused, and what can be done to reduce the number of campus sexual assaults that occur or to eliminate the problem altogether. Wherever the truth may lie regarding campus sexual assault, it is clear that the discussion is far from over.

Opposing Viewpoints: Sexual Assault on Campus examines the complex and controversial matter of college sexual assault in chapters titled "Why Do Sexual Assaults Happen on College Campuses?," "Are College Sexual Assault Cases Being Handled Properly?," "How Might the College Sexual Assault Problem Be Addressed?," and "What Other Factors Are Tied to the Campus Sexual Assault Problem?" This volume offers insight into the serious contemporary issue of sexual assault on campus from an array of different perspectives.

CHAPTER 1

Why Do Sexual Assaults Happen on College Campuses?

Chapter Preface

In recent years, the issue of sexual assault on campus has become an increasingly widespread and pressing concern for colleges across the United States. As activists search for a way to effectively reverse this trend, one question must be asked: Why have college campuses become such hotbeds of sexual violence? Unfortunately, this question has many potential answers and few, if any, that inspire widespread agreement.

By far the easiest target in the search for the root cause of the campus sexual assault crisis is alcohol. It is no secret that college students have a particularly strong penchant for consuming alcohol, sometimes in extreme quantities. As a result, it is equally unsurprising that alcohol consumption plays a role in a large number of on-campus sexual assaults. Whether alcohol consumption is a direct causative factor in the college sexual assault problem, however, is less clear. Although some experts support this conclusion, others do not. The same can be said for the role played by fraternities. While many fraternities encourage aggressive sexual behavior and fraternity parties often involve excessive alcohol consumption, many critics argue that fraternities themselves are not solely, or even principally, responsible for the college sexual assault problem.

That leads to what might be the broadest and most controversial explanation for the campus sexual assault crisis. If practical issues such as alcohol consumption and fraternities are not to blame, some experts contend, then the problem's root cause must be cultural in nature. This philosophy has given rise to the idea that a concept known as "rape culture" is at the heart of the campus sexual assault crisis. According to sociologists and other authorities on social behavior, the term "rape culture" describes societies in which sexual violence is, consciously or otherwise, accepted as a social norm. Supporters of this theory claim that in rape cultures, sexual violence is essentially used as a tool for one gender to assert its dominance over the other. While some, particularly feminists and other activists, assert that rape culture is the true cause of the campus sexual assault crisis, others dismiss this explanation as political propaganda that skews reality and only serves to worsen the problem.

The debate over the existence of rape culture on American college campuses is a divisive one that can have very serious consequences. In November 2014, for example, concerns about college rape culture led to a scandal that significantly impacted the way campus sexual assault is viewed. That month, *Rolling Stone* published a widely read article about "Jackie," a student at the University of Virginia (UVA) who claimed that she had been brutally raped at a fraternity party. Despite the fact that Jackie's claims contained clear inconsistencies and details that could not be verified, *Rolling Stone* editors allowed the story to be published. Almost immediately afterward, it became clear that Jackie's account of what had happened could not have occurred the way she described it and that, according to critics, *Rolling Stone*, without regard for the facts, had jumped at the opportunity to publish a story that would confirm the public's fears about rape culture and sexual assault on college campuses. When the Columbia School of Journalism later reviewed the article, it declared the piece an abject failure of journalism. Further, *Rolling Stone*'s mishandling of the UVA article led many critics to question the merit of how media outlets cover campus sexual assault stories and the broader issues that surround those accounts.

Whether rape culture is or is not a legitimate explanation, the campus sexual assault crisis is a serious issue that must be addressed. For that to happen, further exploration of its root causes is necessary. The authors of the viewpoints in the following chapter examine many potential risk factors that may be to blame for the rise of sexual violence on college campuses across the United States.

> *"Sexual assault involving fraternities is not a new problem. In fact, such assaults are high on the list of insurance claims against fraternities nationwide."*

Fraternities Are Significantly Responsible for the Campus Sexual Assault Problem

Angela Carone

In the following viewpoint, Angela Carone argues that a direct relationship exists between sexual assaults on college campuses and the existence of fraternities. She contends that because of the way such groups are organized and because of the types of parties they hold, fraternities cultivate an environment that enables sexual assault and offers protection for those who commit such acts. Carone is an arts and culture reporter for KPBS in San Diego whose work has appeared in a wide variety of newspapers, magazines, and other publications.

As you read, consider the following questions:

1. According to Carone, why are fraternities hotbeds for sexual assault?

2. According to Carone, why are fraternity members more likely than others to commit sexual assault?

3. Why are the women who are victimized by fraternities often unwilling to come forward and report what happened to them, according to Carone?

At San Diego State University [SDSU], two women have reported sexual assaults at fraternity parties since the beginning of September [2014]. Cal State [California State University] San Marcos is investigating an entire fraternity after multiple similar allegations.

Sexual assault involving fraternities is not a new problem. In fact, such assaults are high on the list of insurance claims against fraternities nationwide. But with the news media, lawmakers and the White House focusing on how universities handle these cases, some believe the culture and norms of campus Greek life will soon get even more scrutiny.

"Right now a lot of attention is being paid to intercollegiate athletics (regarding sexual assaults)," said Peter Lake, a professor of law at Stetson University in Florida. It's only a matter of time, he said, before the focus shifts to another highly visible student group: fraternities. The U.S. Department of Education is investigating how more than 80 schools respond to rape on campus.

Fraternities and Sexual Assault

Experts and Greek insiders agree that a competitive, testosterone-driven environment fueled by alcohol and casual sex is part of fraternities' sexual assault problem. So are the large-scale parties at fraternity houses, which can be ideal surroundings for predatory behavior.

Two studies in 2007 and 2009 published in the *NASPA Journal* suggest that fraternity members are more likely than non-fraternity members to commit rape. One of those studies found that women in sororities are 74 percent more likely to experience rape than other college women.

Victims often don't report rapes at fraternity houses because of fear of retaliation from its members. And brotherhood loyalty pressures some fraternity members to protect known perpetrators. Meanwhile, colleges and universities, along with the national fraternity industry, carefully measure oversight to avoid liability.

Like athletics, fraternities tend to be highly visible at colleges and universities. Their members often sit on student government boards and hold other leadership positions on campus. SDSU has 44 social and cultural fraternities and sororities. UC [University of California] San Diego has 43.

The University of San Diego has 14 fraternities and sororities, comprising 25 percent of the student body. Cal State San Marcos has eight Greek organizations with roughly 500 members.

At SDSU, some fraternity members are trying to change attitudes, little by little. Every semester, 18 to 20 fraternity men cycle through a course called FratMANers, which stands for Fraternity Men Against Negative Environments and Rape Situations.

They spend three hours a week talking about sexual assault, parsing what it means to get consent for sex and describing signs of an assault about to happen. They then give workshops to their peers. The program was founded in 2004 and is part of the school's Student Health Services.

"It's honestly the best class I've taken on this campus," said Wesley Episcopo, a member of Sigma Phi Epsilon, one of SDSU's largest and most popular fraternities.

"It's cool to just bond together and see other fraternity members on the campus who are concerned about this," he said.

The Culture of Fraternities

By their nature, fraternities are competitive. Recruits "rush" fraternities. While philanthropy and leadership opportunities are a thread of Greek life, it's the parties that really make the case to potential pledges.

"There are many, many fraternities across this country where the recruitment process and the idea of what the fraternity provides is access to brotherhood and camaraderie centered around partying and, really, access to women and sex," said Jeff Bucholtz, cofounder of We End Violence, which provides education around sexual violence. Bucholtz also sits on SDSU's newly formed sexual assault task force.

Once inside the fraternity, language and behavior norms can easily send the wrong message, Episcopo said. "There's that big ego part where it's like, yeah, you gotta go out and get laid tonight. And everyone's like yeah, get laid, get lucky, have a good time, and a lot of members take that the wrong way."

They feel pressured to live up to an idealized version of a fraternity brother who gets good grades, is "top dog" on campus and has sex every night of the week, Episcopo said.

Younger fraternity members often need educating, he said.

"They say, well she was asking for it. She was wearing a short skirt, no clothes basically, and she was all themed-out, dressed like a mermaid or whatever," he said.

Fraternities often have themed or costume parties.

"We have to tell them the girls might not feel as if they are being slutty. So we teach them that's someone's sister, that's someone's daughter, that's someone's best friend," Episcopo said.

Then there are the parties themselves.

Episcopo is sometimes on the risk team that works Sigma Phi Epsilon's fraternity parties. He monitors who gets in and who gets cut off from alcohol. He makes sure no one gets hurt.

He rattles off a list: "loud noise, dark, lots of people, plenty of alcohol."

"You know whenever someone talks about a rape situation, they involve those four general topics," said Episcopo.

"If you say those four things, it kinda sounds like a fraternity party."

Bucholtz is quite clear that your average fraternity man is not a rapist. But, he said, when the goal of fraternity parties is to get really drunk and have sex, that gives protective active cover for those who are.

"For a predator, that's an incredibly brilliant space to enter because it's less likely that what you're doing is going to stand out enough to look dangerous," said Bucholtz.

In 2002, David Lisak, then a psychologist at the University of Massachusetts, Boston, [and Paul M. Miller of Brown University School of Medicine] wanted to know more about perpetrators of sexual assaults who are never charged or convicted. Lisak called his study "Repeat Rape [and Multiple Offending Among Undetected Rapists]." He surveyed more than 2,000 men in college. Around 6 percent of those surveyed in Lisak's study had committed rape. The majority of them were repeat offenders.

Lisak recorded a reenactment of an interview transcript with a fraternity member he calls Frank (not his real name). Frank describes how he and his fraternity brothers got freshmen girls to come to parties.

"They were the easiest, like, they didn't know the ropes. They were easy prey," said Frank.

Frank told Lisak they would get girls drunk with a special punch made of hard alcohol and fruit juice. He said there were designated rooms in the fraternity house for sex.

"We'd set aside a few rooms to bring the girls up to when they were ready," Frank said. He then describes sexually assaulting a woman in one of those rooms, even though he clearly didn't think of it as rape.

Fraternity Culture and Sexual Assault

Not every fraternity member is a rapist (nor is every fraternity misogynist). But fraternity members are three times more likely to rape, according to a 2007 study, which notes that fraternity culture reinforces "within-group attitudes" that perpetuate sexual coercion. Taken together, frats and other traditionally male-dominated social clubs crystalize the elements of our culture that reinforce inequality, both gender and otherwise.

Jessica Bennett, "The Problem with Frats Isn't Just Rape. It's Power," Time, December 3, 2014.

The party Frank described was more than 10 years ago but not much has changed, according to interviews with current and recent students and members of the Greek community. Energy drinks and vodka are the preferred concoction at fraternity parties today. At SDSU, party-goers say cocaine and marijuana are both common. And, statistics show, freshmen women are still targets.

Is Anybody Watching?

Journalist Caitlin Flanagan spent a year investigating fraternities for the *Atlantic*. National fraternities buy extensive insurance policies to cover injuries that take place at chapter houses. She said sexual assault is the second most common insurance claim filed against fraternities, after assault and battery.

"It's almost built into the line item budget of the fraternity industry that they're going to get a huge number of sexual assault claims and they need to budget appropriately for that," Flanagan said.

She pointed to a 2010 analysis by a major fraternity insurer that found sexual assaults accounted for 15 percent of the insurance claims filed against fraternities. Flanagan is certain that number understates the problem. Unless a young woman or her parents consult a lawyer, she likely doesn't know it's possible to file an insurance claim against a fraternity.

Further, claiming a rape from within the Greek system can pit a young woman against an entire organization. "Because now she's not just putting herself in conflict with one young man who has assaulted her in a dorm room," Flanagan said. "Now she's putting herself in conflict with a brotherhood of young men who have sworn loyalty to one another for their lifetime."

Those who do speak out about sexual assault in the Greek system are often silenced by other members.

Episcopo, who trains others through the FratMANers program, said the question of reporting rape is hard for many Greek men. During workshops, the question is sometimes posed: "If you had a member who you knew raped a girl, what would you do? Would you send them to the police, understanding that your chapter at large might be in danger?"

"A lot of people said no. They would keep it hush-hush," Episcopo said.

Flanagan said fraternities that have a bad reputation are well known on campuses. However, universities will only go so far in cracking down on them, she said.

"The more supervision and the more control you exercise over the fraternity, the more you establish a legal duty of care," Flanagan said, which means one party has to conform to a certain standard of conduct to protect against unreasonable risk of harm.

"Once you establish a duty of care, when the lawsuit comes in, you're on the line," said Flanagan.

Law professor Peter Lake said the new broader interpretation of Title IX really challenges the long-held practice of universities avoiding a legal duty of care.

Title IX is the 1972 federal law banning sex discrimination in higher education, which includes sexual assault.

"The position the Department of Education seems to take is that the broadly conceived environment in which students live and learn is the orbit of Title IX responsibility," Lake said.

Historically, universities and colleges have viewed their jurisdiction less broadly and more geographically, as in on, off, or close to campus. For example, SDSU's policy covers sexual misconduct by a student with "nexus to campus."

"You can talk about jurisdiction all you want," Lake said. "But Title IX says if you see sex discrimination, you have to respond to it," regardless of the geographical relationship to campus. In other words, in this new era of enforced Title IX compliance, schools might not be able to keep a carefully calibrated distance from what happens at fraternity parties next door to campus.

SDSU requires its fraternities to maintain insurance policies of at least $1 million and to cover the university as part of their policy. After reviewing the policy, Lake said it's not an unusual one but it does "reduce the university from exposure to insurance claims."

Randall Timm, head of SDSU's Student Life and Leadership, said his office regularly advises the fraternities of the various rules they have to follow. If they break the rules, they can face a campus judicial process described as "educational and developmental." Such a process can result in suspension and probation of the entire chapter from university-sanctioned events and support.

SDSU has suspended three fraternities in the past five years for violating its rules.

Combating the Problem

In mid-September, eight national fraternities announced they would band together and create the Fraternal Health & Safety Initiative to combat issues facing fraternities, especially sexual and relationship misconduct, binge drinking and hazing. They are working with an insurer to develop a training program on these topics for their members.

The training is expected to reach more than 35,000 undergraduate students on more than 350 college campuses, including some at SDSU and Cal State San Marcos.

Nancy Sterling, a spokeswoman for the international chapter of Tau Kappa Epsilon [TKE], one of the participating fraternities, said they feel "very strongly that their members live up to a code of conduct."

"Obviously anything involving a sexual assault would be criminal and not in keeping with that code of conduct," added Sterling.

TKE has suspended the San Marcos chapter while Cal State San Marcos conducts its Title IX investigation into multiple sexual assault reports involving the fraternity, which is no longer recognized by the university due to a list of infractions, including hazing and drug and alcohol use. The Title IX coordinator on each campus is charged with investigating sexual assault reports. It's not a criminal investigation, but a student can be expelled if found guilty.

Oceanside [California] police have been conducting a criminal investigation into at least one of the alleged reports since it occurred at a party in their jurisdiction. Detectives had to change tack recently when their only suspect, a TKE member, was cleared through DNA testing.

Phil Ortiz went to SDSU and is a member of Phi Kappa Psi fraternity. He's a former president of FratMANers. He thinks groups like FratMANers can make a difference because it's personal: fraternity brother talking to fraternity brother.

"It's not some university administrator wagging their finger at you," he said.

Ortiz, who led the group six years ago, said the fact that it's still going strong is encouraging.

"It's going to take a lot of effort to change the culture and change the norms, but it's a good place to start," he said.

On Wednesday, members of FratMANers will be handing out teal ribbons at SDSU to raise awareness around sexual violence on the campus. October is within the "Red Zone" on college campuses, a period when rates of sexual assault reports involving freshmen women are statistically higher.

> *"The issue here is that sexual assault is
> not exclusive to the Greek community.
> It is not just a Greek problem; it is a
> campus problem."*

Fraternities Should Not Be Blamed for the Campus Sexual Assault Problem

Blaize Stewart

In the following viewpoint, Blaize Stewart argues that simply placing the blame for campus sexual assaults on fraternities is a misguided and ineffective approach to addressing a very real, very serious problem. He contends that fraternities are only one of many reasons why campus sexual assault has become such a rampant problem and that focusing exclusively on fraternities only leaves other, bigger problems unresolved. Stewart is a writer and editor who has worked extensively for both the Odyssey *and* Impulse Magazine *at the University of Illinois Urbana-Champaign.*

As you read, consider the following questions:

1. Why does Stewart take issue with the title of the *Guardian* article he mentions?

2. According to Stewart, how is the article's approach to the problem of campus sexual assault flawed, and why does this only serve to make the problem worse?

3. According to Stewart, what should colleges be doing to address the problem of campus sexual assault?

When I joined a fraternity, I knew that there would be some who would label me as just another frat guy. They would compare me to the cultural image of the drunken frat star who is barely making it through school with my family credit card and, unless they met me personally, there was nothing I could do to stop them from believing that.

It was difficult to accept that some people would automatically pass judgment just because they saw me wearing Greek letters. Eventually, I learned that is just part of joining a house. However, there is one aspect of fraternity life being broadcast as the norm for fraternity men, which is by no means a trivial issue that can be brushed off.

Blaming Sexual Assault on Fraternities

In a recent article in the *Guardian*, titled "Frat Brothers Rape 300% More. One in 5 Women Sexually Assaulted on Campus. Should We Ban Frats?," a single study is cited as the reason to ban fraternities from every campus.

Before I dive into the ridiculousness of the article, I want to make something very clear: by no means am I trying to defend men who have committed these sexual assaults. In no way am I condoning the behavior of these individuals, or chapters, who have committed these terrible acts. There is no way they should be allowed to remain affiliated with any semblance of Greek life, and they should face the charges they deserve.

The issue here is that sexual assault is not exclusive to the Greek community. It is not just a Greek problem; it is a campus problem. Like I said, fraternity members should be reprimanded and punished as individuals for this, and any chapter that condones this kind of behavior should face similar consequences. But using the entire Greek system as a scapegoat for this issue is not the way to solve the growing problem of sexual assault.

According to an article in the *Washington Post*, 55 percent of about 1,570 colleges and universities with 1,000 or more students received at least one report of forcible sex offense on campus in 2012. Some of the schools on the list, like Reed College [Portland, Oregon] with 9.62 offenses per 1,000 students (2012), have no Greek life. Yet sexual assault is still an issue on their campus.

There are also factors cited, in the article from the *Guardian*, as reasons fraternity men are more likely to commit rape, which are not exclusive to Greek life. For example, having parties and consuming alcohol are considered to be part of why fraternity men are at a higher risk to commit sexual assault. However, what about the several other student organizations and sports teams which also consume alcohol and throw parties? Are they omitted from the stigma of sexual assault because they don't wear Greek letters?

Criticizing the Critics

Right from the start, I had issues with the title of this article because it is poorly written. The article's title gives the impression that fraternity men are the ones committing all these assaults on all the women reporting the crimes. It is misleading in an inappropriate way to skew readers in one direction so they dive into the first paragraph already biased.

Furthermore, the study used as a source was from 2007 and consisted of one freshman class from one university. The broad, overgeneralized statements and conclusions drawn by

Sexual Assault Is Part of a Broader Cultural Problem

Rape is not just a problem among athletes and it is not an incident contained to sorority and fraternity row. Sexual assault is not simply bred within the sectors of our society that oftentimes do have entitlement problems. The rape culture and sexual assault issues we have are the result of a broader cultural mind-set that a human being is something anyone would be entitled to in the first place.

Katie Patton,
"Rape Culture and the Blame Game:
Should We Be Pointing Fingers?,"
Hello Giggles, November 10, 2013.

the writer were vastly exaggerated. Interestingly enough, a study of a similar size, which pulled participants from three Southern universities, found that fraternity men are least likely to be sexually aggressive toward women. But that didn't make the cut for the article.

Going deeper into the article, you can see it is skating over the issue of sexual assault as a national collegiate issue by not holding anyone accountable other than Greek offenders. Should they be held accountable? Absolutely. Should this be the only focus in the discussion of sexual assault? Absolutely not.

By turning this discussion into an issue solely surrounding Greek life, the article is doing a disservice to the past and future victims of sexual assault. It is giving the impression that if we simply ban all Greek life then all sexual assault on campus will disappear, which is clearly not the case.

Solving the Problem

The greater issue here is, what are college campuses doing in order to stop the growing number of sexual assaults? They are the ones who need to be held accountable for the welfare and safety of their students.

In recent news, Columbia [University] student Emma Sulkowicz has been carrying around a twin-sized mattress to protest the way her university handled her sexual assault case. It seems that, in many instances, universities are more concerned with protecting their image and hushing up incidents, rather than dealing with them properly. More often than not, this leads to more pain and suffering for the victims. This cannot be allowed to continue.

Simply blaming fraternities is a lazy, sad attempt to address the issue of sexual assault. It is imperative to make sure schools do everything possible to keep students, Greek and the unaffiliated, educated and aware that sexual assault is a real and persistent issue on college campuses and elsewhere. Perpetuating the idea that the issue can be solved by removing a certain group of people from college campuses takes the discussion on sexual assault nowhere; continuing to do so will only slow the process down unnecessarily while instances of sexual assault rise.

"As a person concerned about sexual violence in our society, and as the mom of a college-age daughter, I care a lot about efforts to dismantle rape culture. Conservative pundits . . . who fret that 'the new rape culture crusade is turning ugly' put primary attention on exactly the wrong thing."

To Fight Campus Rape, Culture Must Change

Barbara J. King

In the following viewpoint, Barbara J. King argues that rape culture is the root of the campus sexual assault problem. As such, she contends that the only way to effectively correct the campus sexual assault crisis is to address the underlying cultural issues from which it arises. With that in mind, she lauds efforts such as Wesleyan College's move to establish coed fraternities to foster sexual equality. King is a professor of anthropology at the College of William and Mary and an expert in animal behavior and human evolution.

As you read, consider the following questions:

1. According to King, what were her initial concerns about measures by the California legislature and Wesleyan College to curb campus sexual assault?

2. According to Peggy Reeves Sanday, how would these measures help to change the culture of college campuses in relation to sex and sexual assault?

3. According to Sanday, widespread sexual aggression is often related to what?

Inside Higher Ed reports this week [in June 2014] on a California bill that would require college students to obtain "an affirmative, unambiguous, and conscious decision by each participant to engage in mutually agreed-upon sexual activity."

The bill, already approved by California's Senate, is a response to escalating concerns about rape culture on college campuses. As *Inside Higher Ed* notes:

> "The proposal would shift the burden of proof in campus sexual assault cases in which the accused cites consent as the defense to those accused, rather than those making the allegations."

A second recent proposal, this time aimed at campus policy rather than state mandate, comes from Wesleyan College in Connecticut. There, a group of faculty, staff, and students propose the coed integration of campus fraternities, so that women would live alongside men in them. Noting the climate of sexual assault that is linked with fraternities, the creators of the proposal write that educational efforts must be by fraternities and not merely aimed at them:

> "The societies themselves must substantially co-educate, affording equal privilege and control to individuals of all genders, in order to eliminate the gender-based power dynamics by which sexual assault is promoted within fraternities.

Moreover, drastic and continuous reform to practices and culture within fraternities is needed to adequately address the rape culture they explicitly or implicitly endorse."

As a person concerned about sexual violence in our society, and as the mom of a college-age daughter, I care a lot about efforts to dismantle rape culture. Conservative pundits like Christina Hoff Sommers who fret that "the new rape culture crusade is turning ugly" put primary attention on exactly the wrong thing. Vigilance against false accusations is necessary, sure, but Sommers' suggestion of "paranoia" is a stunning dismissal of the statistical realities.

And when George Will [of the *Washington Post*] suggested a few days ago that when colleges "make victimhood a coveted status that confers privileges, victims proliferate," responses have been appropriately pointed, as in this column by Zerlina Maxwell ["Rape Isn't a Privilege, It's an Epidemic," MSNBC, June 10, 2014].

Something has to change on our campuses.

Originally, I worried about the efficacy of the measures suggested in California and at Wesleyan. Won't the California bill just lead to more he-said, she-said confrontations? (Men are raped, too, and rape occurs also outside a male-female context; but today I focus on the statistical-majority problem.) If the male aggressor claims that the female "partner" gave spoken consent, would the woman be believed? And on the matter of fraternities, is it really safe to ask women to integrate them? Could such a social experiment not be costly physically and emotionally to the women who pioneer the change?

In seeking guidance, I could think of no one more informed to consult than the anthropologist Peggy Reeves Sanday, whose writings—including the book *Fraternity Gang Rape: Sex, Brotherhood, and Privilege on Campus*—focus on sexual violence in the U.S. and cross culturally.

Rape Culture and Sexual Aggression

Beyond the act of physical and sexual violence, posttrau-matic rape syndrome, as well as the refusal of many rape victims to report when they have been assaulted, can be attributed to a prevailing rape culture on America's college campuses. Rape culture is a term used to describe the way rape, sexual violence, and sexual abuse are linked to the culture of society. Essentially sexual violence and speech against women is normalized and excused in media and pop culture. Thus, male sexual aggression is in a number of ways encouraged and supported in society.

Cherise Charleswell,
"Boys Will Be Boys: America's Campus Rape Policy,"
The Hampton Institute, July 2, 2014.

In an email message, Sanday responded with thoughts that made me feel more hopeful about both measures. On the matter of fraternities, a case-study experience of Sanday's brought good news:

"I have worked with a fraternity at the University of Pennsylvania that lost its charter and then sought to regroup as a coed fraternity. I was impressed with the dedication of the brothers and the women they worked with who came to live at their house. It was clear that they didn't have the mentality that parties were only about 'getting laid.' At parties, they appointed designated watchers to question male and female party guests or house members who appeared unable to function due to drinking. What impressed me in talking to male and female house members was the degree to which they showed concern for everyone."

Sanday highlighted the importance of "the fact that college males are directly questioning the privileging of the all-male spaces that often rule campus party life."

Reflecting on both the California and Wesleyan proposals, Sanday had this to say:

"These two developments—enforceable legal guidelines favoring evidence of affirmative consent on some campuses together with the critical examination of fraternity life on many campuses—promise to make campus sexual cultures more equitable and by so doing change the broader understanding of the meaning of sexual equality."

Sanday also made points about the plasticity of human behavior as regards sexual violence that were relevant:

"Also useful is the serious reexamination of the U.S. cultural privileging of male sexual aggression on the grounds that because it is 'natural' it cannot be questioned. Anthropological research and fieldwork, including my own, dispute this assumption. There is wide variability in sexual customs ranging from societies in which sexual aggression is rare to those in which it is common."

"In my own work I differentiate such societies as rape-free as opposed to rape-prone. Looking at ninety-five band and tribal societies, I found that forty-seven percent could be classified as rape-free, while only eighteen percent were rape-prone. By rape-free I did not imply that there was no rape, only that there was a very low incidence compared to rape-prone societies in which the aggressive assault of women was a common component of male sexual culture and was not punished. Interestingly, widespread sexual aggression is often related to a social emphasis on male toughness and competition and a low respect for women as citizens. In the rape-free societies I studied, rape is punished and both sexes hold exalted positions in public decision making and both are integrated and equal in the affairs of everyday life."

"Such findings suggest that whatever the biological component might be in sexual expression, cultural values and social policies make a difference. In other words, as much as college policies can nurture sexual equality, their absence can have the result of nurturing sexual inequality."

Sanday's last point merits extra emphasis. I know of no research on this question specifically, but over and over again in my informal networks I hear of students who feel that the administration at their colleges don't really want to hear what's going on and don't make it easy to report and follow through on incidents of sexual violence.

These two proposed measures will not end rape culture. But something has to change. As the proponents of the Wesleyan proposal write, "We reject a course of inaction simply because action is imperfect."

> "With all of the attention focused on the exaggerated claims of a sexual assault culture, the very real problem of the hookup culture on these campuses—including some Catholic campuses—is ignored."

The Campus Sexual Assault Problem Is Not the Result of "Rape Culture"

Anne Hendershott

In the following viewpoint, Anne Hendershott argues that the so-called "rape culture" on American college campuses is an exaggerated and inaccurate characterization that has gained widespread traction only because it has triggered a misguided moral panic. Further, she alleges that the real problem behind college sexual assault is the hookup culture and the lack of a moral community on most campuses. Hendershott is a sociology professor at Franciscan University and the author of Status Envy: The Politics of Catholic Higher Education, The Politics of Abortion, *and* The Politics of Deviance.

As you read, consider the following questions:

1. According to Hendershott, why is it clear that the supposed campus sexual assault crisis is false?

2. According to Hendershott, why is the current response to the campus sexual assault crisis only going to make the problem worse?

3. According to Hendershott, what should be done to make college campuses safer?

Undeterred by data debunking the notion that college campuses have become what Senator Kirsten Gillibrand (D-NY) has called "havens for rape and sexual assault," the [Barack] Obama administration is now investigating 90 colleges and universities for possible alleged sexual violence. Suggesting that "women are at a greater risk of sexual assault as soon as they step onto a college campus," Senator Gillibrand introduced the Campus Accountability and Safety Act last summer.

The Rape Culture Moral Panic

The only problem is that much of what is reported about a so-called "epidemic" of campus sexual assault is false. A study released last month [November 2014] by the Bureau of Justice Statistics revealed that the rate of rape and other sexual assault over the past two decades was 1.2 times higher for non-students of college age than for students on college campuses. In fact, campus sexual assault has actually declined from 9.2 per 1,000 college students in 1997 to 4.4 per 1,000 in 2013. Far from being a site of violence, the study found that female college students are safer from sexual assault while in college than at any other time in their lives.

Yet, hostage to the largesse of the federal government through student aid and federal grants, campus administrators have been forced to implement mandatory sexual assault workshops for students, faculty, and support staff. These are new federal requirements under Title IX—the gender equity law created in 1972 to protect individuals from discrimination based on sex in education. These requirements are mandated for all colleges and universities—including Catholic colleges and universities. Led by attorneys and representatives of a newly created sexual assault industry of victims' advocates, faculty are warned that when credible allegations of sexual assault arise, the alleged perpetrator is barred from classes and campus events. And, in the moral panic surrounding sexual assault, any allegation is a credible allegation as punitive policies are implemented infringing on the civil rights of men.

Claiming that campus sexual assault is a common phenomenon, the promoters of the panic have attempted to deploy the allegations of campus sexual assault against political opponents in what they see as evidence of the "war on women." Senator Gillibrand, a major promoter of the panic, moved on to campus sexual assault after targeting what she called a military culture of "violence and power" last spring. In March, Gillibrand demanded that the military chain of command be replaced with civilian legal processes in cases of sexual harassment and assault in the military—claiming that the military leadership is unable to deal with these issues. Citing the now-discredited statistic that 26,000 service members were sexually assaulted last year, panicked prosecutors and military leaders initiated some of the most preposterous prosecutions we have seen—until the tide of false sex abuse allegations on college campuses began to reach its height last fall.

Politics always plays the pivotal role in any moral panic—especially a panic involving women portrayed as victims of a patriarchal culture. Exaggerated claims by advocates like Gillibrand and her sexual assault industry supporters are coupled with incendiary headlines in the media. Promoting the military sexual assault panic, the *New York Times* editorialized that the sexual assaults are the result of the "military's entrenched culture of sexual violence."

43

The Rape Culture Crusade

Sexual assault on campus is a genuine problem—but the new rape culture crusade is turning ugly. This movement is turning our campuses into hostile environments for free expression and due process. And so far, university officials, political leaders, and the White House are siding with the mob.

Christina Hoff Sommers,
"Rape Culture Is a 'Panic Where Paranoia, Censorship,
and False Accusations Flourish,'" Time, May 15, 2014.

Those who dare question the existence of the "epidemic" of sexual assault on college campuses and military bases are vilified. Following the publication last spring of a *Wall Street Journal* column suggesting the possibility of a panic surrounding sexual assault, Terry O'Neill, president of NOW [National Organization for Women], called on the newspaper to fire author James Taranto because he is "determined to maintain or even deepen the rape culture that pervades campuses and much of society."

And, when columnist George Will published a column in the *Washington Post* last June suggesting that when campuses "make victimhood a coveted status that confers privileges, victims proliferate," he was uninvited from speaking at Scripps College. Will is scheduled to provide the commencement address at Michigan State [University (MSU)], but MSU president Lou Anna Simon issued a statement explaining that he was selected as speaker before he wrote the controversial June column. Simon added that having Will speak "does not mean the university wishes to cause survivors of sexual assault distress."

The Hookup Culture Is the Real Problem

With all of the attention focused on the exaggerated claims of a sexual assault culture, the very real problem of the hookup culture on these campuses—including some Catholic campuses—is ignored. In "'Hooking Up' at College: Does Religion Make a Difference?," an article in the *Journal for the Scientific Study of Religion* that appeared a few years ago [2009], sociology professors Amy Burdette, Terrence Hill, Christopher Ellison and Norval Glenn described the results of a comparative study of the dating behavior of college students. Drawing from a national sample of 1,000 college women, the sociologists surveyed female college students in an effort to analyze the influence of both individual and institutional religious factors on engaging in casual sexual encounters. The results revealed that "hooking up" has replaced traditional forms of courtship on college campuses and appears to be a reflection of the changing norms in the dating and sexual behaviors of college students.

In their study, Burdette attempted to point to the role that "moral communities" have historically played in the lives of students. They hypothesized that those communities with shared moral convictions would have a strong moral influence on students. Predicting that Catholic campuses, for example, would have a moralizing influence on their students, Burdette and her colleagues were surprised to learn when they analyzed their survey data that this was not the case on the Catholic campuses they studied.

Although the goal of the study was to determine whether or not religious affiliation and activity would make a difference in the students' decision to participate in casual sex, the authors found that "not all religiously affiliated colleges and universities constitute moral communities." In fact, on several of the Catholic campuses they studied, a "moral community" was completely missing. While women enrolled in Evangelical Protestant colleges were much less likely to participate in the hookup culture, women enrolled in Catholic colleges were more likely to have "hooked up" while at school than women at colleges with no religious affiliation.

While the sample size was not adequate to make generalizations about the hookup culture on all Catholic campuses, and the authors did not control for "faithfulness" of the campus culture on hooking-up behavior, the results suggest that the hookup culture is common on some Catholic college campuses. And, more importantly, the women surveyed are unhappy with the role they have been pressured to play in the hookup culture that has developed on their campuses.

The hookup culture is real—and it is likely that there is a link between the hookup culture and the panic over sexual assault on college campuses. Sadly, the response to the sexual assault panic will do little to change this culture as the "protective" policies actually end up removing power from women—creating instead, female children unable to stand up for themselves and in need of protection by the now-entrenched sex codes created by college campus feminists. Remoralizing the campus can happen. For instance, Catholic University has reinstated single-sex dorms in an attempt to help students create a healthier culture. Other campuses are implementing similar kinds of programs. Creating moral communities should be the goal for all Catholic college leaders.

> "I thought it was a progressive school. I thought the resources they advertised from the beginning were real resources I could count on. I felt even more betrayed when they failed me and then refused to acknowledge my earnest desires and pleas for them to evaluate what was happening to me."

Columbia Student Carrying Mattress to Protest Alleged Rape Gets 'Overwhelmingly Positive' Response

Eun Kyung Kim

In the following viewpoint, Eun Kyung Kim, through an interview with college rape survivor Emma Sulkowicz, characterizes the campus sexual assault problem as the result of administrative failure. In the interview, Sulkowicz shares her assault story and explains that her decision to carry a mattress around the Columbia University campus is an expression of her frustration

Eun Kyung Kim, "Columbia Student Carrying Mattress to Protest Alleged Rape Gets 'Overwhelmingly Positive' Response," *Today News*, September 5, 2014. Copyright © 2014 NBC News. All rights reserved. Reproduced with permission.

with the school administration's failure to properly address her situation. *Kim is an Arizona-based writer who contributes to TODAY.com and other news outlets.*

As you read, consider the following questions:

1. According to Sulkowicz, why did she choose to carry around a mattress as a demonstration?

2. According to Sulkowicz, how long does she intend to continue carrying the mattress?

3. Sulkowicz says what has been the most difficult part of her demonstration?

Emma Sulkowicz has been carrying a heavy load ever since starting classes Tuesday at Columbia University. Literally.

The visual arts senior has brought a twin-sized dorm mattress everywhere she goes and plans to continue lugging it around until her alleged rapist gets kicked off campus. She says it's a statement about the way the university has handled the situation, as well as a work of art, which will serve as her senior thesis project.

Sulkowicz said she was assaulted in her dorm room by a classmate on the first day of her sophomore year. She accuses Columbia administrators of mishandling the investigation into the incident, and has protested the dismissal of her case against the assailant, particularly as two other women have claimed they also were raped by the same man in separate incidents.

On the fourth day of what Sulkowicz calls "Mattress Performance/Carry That Weight," she spoke with TODAY.com about her project, the widespread attention it has received and the tremendous encouragement coming from her coeds.

TODAY: *Did you expect to get such a response?*

Emma Sulkowicz: I wasn't expecting it to blow up this big. It's been an overwhelmingly positive response in terms of everyone that I know. Most of the negative responses have pretty much been limited to the Internet and grumpy commenters on blogs. And then there's the reporters' response—I've never had this much reporter attention before, so it's kind of frightening because I'm being watched so much, but it's also a sign that people care, so it's also a good thing.

TODAY: Have you had to carry the mattress around by yourself?

ES: I've only had one trip so far where no one has helped me at all, and I think it was because I was being flocked by reporters, which is pretty intimidating for a lot of people. I've met a lot of people just by us all holding the mattress and talking together while we're walking to places.

TODAY: Do most people who come up to you know why you're carrying a mattress?

ES: Most people help me because they know why I'm carrying it, yet I've gotten some pretty annoying reactions from people who don't know why. I've had four men come up to me and be like, "Oh I just want to lie down on your mattress." And that's the opposite reason of why I'm carrying it. It's some weird way of flirting with me, and, of course, it's not what I want to hear.

TODAY: How did you come up with the idea?

ES: I was working on an art piece (over the summer) at the Yale Norfolk Art Residency and I had to move a mattress out of a room to make a video. The image of me moving a mattress got stuck in my head. I think it was because I was raped in my own bed—it was a place associated with a lot of pain and hurt. The idea of me having to carry around my pain everywhere I go was reflected in me bringing the mattress, which is kept in a safe place, out into the light and into the public eye. That mirrored the situation I was in and I felt like it was a good metaphor.

TODAY: Is your effort being interpreted correctly by the media and the public?

49

ES: I'm glad that people are moved by it, which is really important to me. I think a lot of news stations have been portraying it as a protest, my protest, but to me, it's my artwork and something I've been considering an art piece. I saw one debate recently that Dr. Drew [Pinsky] held on his TV show, where one man was arguing that I had artistic motivations in this piece. I was like, "Well, yeah—I'm making an art piece and that's the whole point."

TODAY: Do you really plan to carry the mattress around until your school takes action?

ES: Yes. I plan on carrying it until I don't go to school with my rapist anymore.

TODAY: Have you seen him on campus?

ES: I saw him on campus before school started, but I haven't seen him since.

TODAY: Has this past week been therapeutic for you?

ES: Not yet. Right now I'm still shocked by the amount of press it's gotten and that this is really happening. Everything feels so surreal right now. I haven't really even gotten a chance to digest my emotions at all, but I think over time when everything starts to settle, I'll be able to reevaluate.

TODAY: Have you heard from the Columbia administration?

ES: They haven't said anything to me yet. I saw (the college dean) yesterday, the one who flat-out denied my appeal, and it was amazing. He turned his entire body into a question mark. He was staring at his feet. He would not look up. He wouldn't acknowledge that this giant mattress was walking by.

TODAY: Are you holding your college up to higher standards because it's an Ivy League school?

ES: Yes. I thought it was a progressive school. I thought the resources they advertised from the beginning were real resources I could count on. I felt even more betrayed when they failed me and then refused to acknowledge my earnest desires and pleas for them to evaluate what was happening to me and how poorly I was being treated by the (administrative) hearing panel. It's just been amazing how the bureaucracy has stifled me at what's supposed to be such a progressive and liberal school.

TODAY: Has it been emotionally painful or helpful to continually publicize your attack?

ES: The most painful thing for me has been dealing with people who doubt me and think, "Oh she's doing this art piece, she must be lying." Or, "This never happened to her. She's a (expletive) slut. She's a liar." All the people somehow are using the attention I've gotten to discredit me. I know what happened. Why would I lie about something that terrible? That's been the most painful thing—dealing with people who don't believe something that was really traumatic for me.

TODAY: Are you carrying around your actual mattress?

ES: I can't take my dorm room mattress around with me because the Columbia occupancy agreement says that we're not allowed to bring furniture out of the room, so I contacted the mattress provider for Columbia University to purchase my own.

> *"Colleges need to partner with students to examine current alcohol policies and develop programs that reduce hazardous levels of drinking."*

What's Alcohol Got to Do with It?

Antonia Abbey

In the following viewpoint, Antonia Abbey investigates the relationship between campus sexual assault and the consumption of alcohol. She concludes that alcohol can, indeed, increase sexual aggression and lead to sexual misconduct. Based on her findings, Abbey also asserts that colleges and students should work together to reduce alcohol consumption on campus and encourage males to view women as equal sexual partners. Abbey is a psychology professor and an expert in women's health and domestic violence who specializes in issues related to alcohol and sexual assault.

As you read, consider the following questions:

1. According to Abbey, what roles might alcohol play in relation to sexual aggressiveness?

2. According to Abbey, why does the consumption of alcohol encourage violent behavior in those who are already predisposed to sexual aggression?

3. What did Abbey discover about the amount of alcohol a person consumes and the likelihood that he or she will commit an act of sexual aggression?

We've all read the headlines: Sexual assault is disturbingly commonplace across the United States, with college campuses currently receiving intense scrutiny for Title IX violations, their policies regarding sexual assault allegations, and their treatment of victims. Many of the stories we hear on the news involve intoxicated male perpetrators and female victims. It is easy to understand why people wonder if many of these sexual assaults could be avoided if no one was drinking. But what's the evidence? Does alcohol play a causal role in men's sexual violence against women?

As is true for most human behavior, the answer is complicated. About half of all sexual assaults involve alcohol consumption by the perpetrator or victim or both. (Here we refer to sexual assault as the full range of forced sexual acts, including forced touching and kissing, verbally coerced intercourse, and physically forced vaginal, oral and anal penetration.) When alcohol is involved, it may play one of three roles, and there is evidence that each is sometimes true.

Alcohol may encourage sexual aggression—in specific situations, among individuals predisposed to sexual aggression.

Conversely, sexual aggression may cause alcohol consumption. Wait, isn't that backward? No: Some perpetrators may get drunk to justify sexual aggression.

Drinking and sexual aggression can co-occur, because they are both caused by other factors. For example, an underlying personality trait such as impulsivity might lead someone to drink alcohol and to commit sexual assault.

Why are these distinctions important? Because different prevention and treatment programs are needed to address these different situations. Interventions that limit alcohol consumption are likely to be most effective when alcohol plays a causal role. For perpetrators who are using alcohol as an excuse for violence, programs are needed that discredit that notion so they will be held legally and morally responsible for their actions. Perpetrators with underlying personality disorders may need intensive psychotherapy.

What Kind of Person Would Commit a Sexual Assault?

Evidence shows that men who commit sexual violence against women tend to score high on a number of characteristics that put them at risk for sexual aggression. Perpetrators vary; no one set of risk factors describes them all. But many show a strong lack of concern for other people, scoring high on narcissism and low on empathy. Many have high levels of anger in general as well as hostility toward women; they are suspicious of women's motives, believe common rape myths (e.g., women say "no" when they mean "yes"), and have a sense of entitlement about sex. Many also prefer casual sexual relationships and drink heavily.

According to the research, men with many of these risk factors are most likely to commit sexual violence. Thus, even when alcohol plays a causal role, it doesn't work alone. Instead, it works in combination with personality, attitudes and past experience.

Are Drinking Perpetrators Different?

A few studies have compared perpetrators who drank during a sexual assault with those who did not. They found that both drinking and sober perpetrators had similar scores on many of the risk factors described above.

The two groups did differ in their degree of alcohol consumption. Perpetrators who committed an alcohol-involved sexual assault were the heaviest drinkers, both in general and in potential sexual situations with women. They also strongly believed that alcohol increased their own sex drive and that alcohol made women want to have sex.

So alcohol appears, primarily, to influence the circumstances under which some men are most likely to commit sexual assault, but not to influence who will become a perpetrator in the first place. This sets the stage for the next point.

Body and Mind

Alcohol consumption hits us from two directions: Pharmacologically, alcohol is a drug that affects brain function, and psychologically, it is associated with common assumptions about alcohol use.

Pharmacologically, alcohol impairs a host of cognitive functions: episodic and working memory, abstract reasoning, planning and judgment. This set of functions is often labeled "executive cognitive functioning" and is used to weigh conflicting information and make complex decisions. Alcohol also impedes inhibitions, leading people to focus on what is most salient and ignore harder-to-access motives such as empathy for the victim and concern for future consequences. It can also exaggerate anger, frustration, sexual arousal and entitlement, especially among men predisposed to sexual aggression.

Psychologically, many cultures glamorize alcohol consumption and link it to disinhibition, sexual desire, sexual performance, risk taking and aggression. As on Mardi Gras or New Year's Eve, alcohol provides a time-out from normal rules. It is easier to excuse inappropriate behavior when drinking, allowing some men to act on their sexual arousal and sense of entitlement by pushing a woman for sex regardless of her response. When she refuses his advances, it doesn't take much to trigger an aggressive response for some.

It All Works Together

Sex and alcohol are frequently linked in movies, music lyrics and advertisements. These beliefs are often outside conscious awareness; nonetheless, they influence how we perceive other people and their actions. For example, some studies ask sober individuals to read a story about a couple on a date. Nothing about the story varies except what the woman in the story is drinking. When she is described as having two drinks of alcohol, she is viewed by others as behaving more sexually and being more interested in having sex as compared with when she consumed two sodas.

Beliefs can take on a life of their own. Thus, if someone predisposed to sexual aggression decides a drinking woman is interested in having sex, he is much more likely to ignore refusals, assuming she is just "playing hard to get." If he is also drinking, then alcohol-induced cognitive impairments allow him to focus only on his sexual gratification and to feel justified in using force. These beliefs do not warrant the use of sexual violence or lessen perpetrators' responsibility for their actions. But we need to understand perpetrators' justifications for their actions in order to develop effective prevention and treatment programs.

Here's a Hypothetical . . .

It is nearly impossible (and unethical) for researchers to observe situations in which sexual aggression is likely to occur. Thus, researchers bring people into their labs and randomly assign some to drink an alcoholic beverage and some to drink a nonalcoholic beverage. Male participants are then exposed to scenarios that describe a prototypical campus sexual assault: The man and woman know each other, they engage in some consensual sexual activity, but when the woman refuses further sexual activity, the man uses verbal and physical pressure to obtain sex against her will.

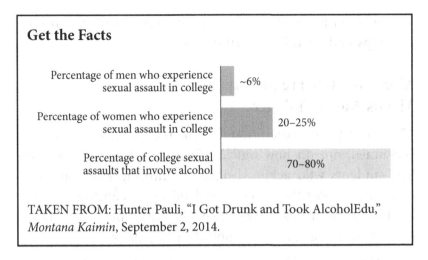

Get the Facts

Percentage of men who experience sexual assault in college ~6%

Percentage of women who experience sexual assault in college 20–25%

Percentage of college sexual assaults that involve alcohol 70–80%

TAKEN FROM: Hunter Pauli, "I Got Drunk and Took AlcoholEdu," *Montana Kaimin*, September 2, 2014.

When compared with sober participants, intoxicated participants evaluate the man's behavior as more appropriate and less violent, are more likely to believe the woman enjoyed being forced to have sex, and report greater willingness to use similar strategies if they were in similar situations.

For example, one study asked 160 male college students to listen to an audiotape of a date rape in which the woman agrees to kissing and touching but protests when the man attempts to remove her clothes. The female character's refusals become more and more vehement as the tape progresses, and the male character uses escalating levels of verbal and physical force.

Participants were asked to stop the tape at the point the male character's behavior was inappropriate and he should leave the woman alone. Participants who consumed alcohol allowed the man to continue for a longer period of time and rated the woman's sexual arousal higher than did sober participants. The findings suggest that intoxicated men may project their own sexual arousal onto a woman, missing or ignoring her active protest.

Other studies have found that alcohol's effects are strongest among men who are predisposed to sexual aggression due to their high levels of hostility, acceptance of violence in relationships and need for sexual dominance.

More Alcohol Frequently Means More Violence

Most surveys of sexual assault focus on whether alcohol was consumed, not on how much. When we asked 113 male college students who acknowledged committing a sexually violent act to report the number of drinks they consumed before or during the incident, we discovered that the more alcohol consumed, the greater the amount of aggression.

Based on the tactics used and the type of sex that was forced (ranging from verbally coerced sexual contact to physically forced penetrative sex), we found that as perpetrators' alcohol consumption increased from zero to four drinks, outcome severity also increased. It then plateaued until nine drinks were consumed. No surprise: At that level, perpetrators' cognitive and motor impairments were presumably too debilitating for them to complete a rape.

Moving Forward

As this brief summary of the research highlights, there is no simple answer to the question, "Does alcohol cause sexual aggression?" Research verifies that men behave more aggressively when drinking; however, the effects appear to be strongest for people who are already predisposed to aggression. The personality characteristics, attitudes and past experiences of sexual assault perpetrators who drink before and during the assault are similar to those who do not.

Heavy episodic drinking contributes to many problems for college students in addition to increasing the risk of sexual assault. Multiple approaches to prevention and treatment are needed to counteract alcohol's psychological and pharmacological effects. Colleges need to partner with students to examine current alcohol policies and develop programs that reduce hazardous levels of drinking.

It is also time to consider the insidious negative effects of media images that link alcohol with sexual desire and continue to encourage men's use of women as sexual objects rather than equal partners. Educators have the opportunity to encourage students to carefully evaluate these messages and to make their own decisions about responsible alcohol consumption and sexual behavior.

> "It's not more drinking that's to blame
> for more sexual assaults, because drink-
> ing hasn't changed. What has changed
> is that there is just a lot more unstruc-
> tured interaction between young men
> and young women."

Is Alcohol Really to Blame for the Prevalence of Sexual Assault on College Campuses?

Daniel Luzer

In the following viewpoint, Daniel Luzer argues that alcohol is not to blame for the ongoing campus sexual assault problem. Instead, he asserts that the real root cause of the problem is the unrestricted interaction male and female students enjoy in today's college environment. In short, he believes that if students had fewer opportunities for cross-gender mingling, fewer opportunities for sexual violence would arise. Luzer is a writer and an editor who serves as the news editor of Governing *magazine. He also has contributed to publications including* Columbia Journalism Review, Mother Jones, *and* Pacific Standard.

As you read, consider the following questions:

1. According to Luzer, why is telling female college students to avoid drinking for their safety perceived as wrong?

2. According to Luzer, for how long has drinking been a prevalent activity on college campuses?

3. What was the "parietal," and how did it impact the way male and female college students interacted with one another when it was in force?

Many Americans are concerned about sexual assault on college campuses. While the number of those affected is still being debated (one in four is commonly cited), even the conservative estimate is that some one in 50 women are made the victims of rape while in college.

Why does sexual assault occur so often? There are a number of elements to consider, but, according to the 2007 "Campus Sexual Assault Study" published by the U.S. Department of Justice, "alcohol consumption by the victim is a major risk factor for sexual assault."

But is drinking really the cause of many sexual assault cases, and the reason for its prevalence on college campuses? Historically this seems questionable. If there has been any change at all in sexual assault patterns at institutions of higher learning—and that the numbers are climbing is one fact that isn't up for debate—it can't be explained by alcohol consumption, which has remained pretty constant. What has changed is the way that men and women socialize.

In a controversial column, *Slate*'s Emily Yoffe noted that a whole lot of these sexual assaults occur in the aftermath of large parties, where everyone is drunk. As she wrote:

A common denominator in these cases is alcohol, often copious amounts, enough to render the young woman incapacitated. But a misplaced fear of blaming the victim has made it somehow unacceptable to warn inexperienced young women that when they get wasted, they are putting themselves in potential peril.

Tell the women not to drink so much, she concludes.

But as Tyler Kingkade put it at the *Huffington Post*, it's mostly drunk boys who are, after all, assaulting those drunk girls. So "let's tell men not to get drunk as sexual assault prevention," he wrote. Since those responsible for the assaults are also drunk, maybe it makes more sense to tell *them* not to drink. But the problem may not be the alcohol at all: "in terms of stopping sexual violence, let's start with teaching people not to rape and go from there."

Seriously? No one's warning women that bad things happen when they drink? I seem to remember the "getting drunk is dangerous" theme being pretty central to all of those orientation meetings I went to (along with women) my freshman year of college. There were posters in every hallway to back up these messages.

A lot of people found Yoffe's column—and advice—offensive.

Katie McDonough responded at *Salon* the very next day. "[W]omen's behavior is the real reason they are victimized—and that we live in a society that does a poor job of policing such behavior—is regularly used to blame sexual violence on the 'problem' of young women," she wrote. Telling women to avoid getting drunk as a way to avoid sexual assault implies that rape is somehow their fault.

Over time colleges have reported an increase in sexual assaults. A 2010 article in the *Washington Examiner* explained that "women are increasingly being victimized on college campuses across the Washington region" and "five out of eight" campuses in the area indicated an increase in sexual offenses committed from 2007 to 2008. Other regions relate similar increases, and seem to indicate more every year. This is a long-term trend. Colleges had few reported rapes 20 or 30 years ago, and many reported sexual assaults in recent years.

Sexual assault is, oddly enough, a recent development on college campuses, but students have been drinking for a long time, and often quite heavily. University students were famous for their drunkenness even in the ancient world.

The National Survey on Drug Use and Health shows that just under 40 percent of people between the ages of 18 and 25 binge on alcohol, down slightly from about 42 percent in 2003. About 40 percent of people in college have always been heavy drinkers; surveys conducted since the early 1980s show similar patterns.

It's true that alcohol is usually involved in college sexual assault cases and therefore it may be a good idea to reduce consumption, but just telling people, male or female, not to drink so much probably isn't going to do very much because college students *like* to get drunk.

And they like to get drunk everywhere. Research from 2007 published in *Current Opinion in Psychiatry* indicated that college drinking was not a problem unique to the United States: "The prevalence of hazardous drinking [among young people] in Australasia, Europe, and South America appears similar to that in North America."

But something about this is wrong. While we've seen a vast increase in reporting of sexual assault on college campuses over the last 50 years, there's been no noticeable change in alcohol consumption. So what's really going on?

A few years ago I had an internship in which I worked for an older man who had a rather senior position at the State Department. At one point—I was in college then—we were talking about how college students party. He graduated from Yale, and when he was younger apparently he and his friends would routinely go up to Poughkeepsie to hang out with the Vassar girls. He, who had attended college in the late '50s, said that it was really quite a task, back when he was younger, driving back to New Haven "late at night, in the dark, when you were pretty drunk."

At the time, Vassar was a women's college and Yale was a men's college. Well into the 1970s, gender segregated schools were common.

Even at your average coed state school, the domestic arrangements of men and women were largely separate. Men and women still socialized, still drank heavily, and still had plenty of sex, of course, but the stumbling over to the nearest frat party, getting blisteringly drunk, and then going back to your dorm thing—you just didn't do that the same way.

There are also more women in college than ever before. Total enrollment statistics indicate that women outnumbered men for the first time in the late 1970s, and their numbers have steadily increased since then. Women have represented about 57 percent of enrollments at American colleges since at least the year 2000.

Coeducation became standard in the late 20th century, but there were intricate rules about gender interaction until the 1980s. According to Otis Gates, a Harvard graduate:

> For the Class of 1956, parietals—the hours when women were allowed in male dormitories—restricted how they interacted with the opposite sex. According to the rules, women could be in male dormitories until 11 P.M. on Saturdays and from 4 to 7 P.M. on weekdays for upperclassmen....

> ... As members of the Class of 1956 completed their freshman year, they lost the opportunity to entertain women from 1 to 4 P.M., in return for a three-hour extension on Saturday evenings until 11 P.M. Despite the gain on Saturday nights, undergraduates had a net loss of 15 hours per week of parietal hours.

During the "parietal" (a word no longer found anywhere on the average college campus) hours, women were often allowed in men's rooms but the doorway had to be open "the width of a book." (Many students cleverly interpreted this to mean a matchbook.)

Things were very different then. At many private, and even public, colleges there were rules about church attendance and clothing, too, such that "male students were required to wear clean and neat dress slacks (no jeans or shorts), dress shirts (no T-shirts, knit shirts, plaids, or bold stripes), and dress shoes (no slippers, tennis shoes, clogs, or thongs)" to dinner. Many freshmen couldn't take cars to school based on the belief that "they could be a potential distraction from their course work."

In such a world, how many drinks you had didn't matter as much; sexual assault is less likely to happen if people don't even think about going home together.

These rules often come up in discussions with older alumni: "Things were so strict back then; you kids had it easy!" But this isn't incidental. The Justice Department study indicates that students "who resided in sorority houses and on-campus dormitories were more likely to report experiencing rape than students residing off campus." And furthermore "freshmen and sophomore women appear to be at greater risk of being victims of sexual assault than are upperclassmen." And that's just because, well, they're more likely to live around them.

None of this, of course, excuses anyone's behavior. As Gates so succinctly put it in an interview he did for a story in Harvard's campus newspaper, "This is not to say that one's interest with the other sex was any different than it is now, but there was a different way that people were expected to interact." It's probably true that if no one got drunk we'd see a lot fewer sexual assaults. But it's not more drinking that's to blame for more sexual assaults, because drinking hasn't changed. What has changed is that there is just a lot more unstructured interaction between young men and young women.

Periodical and Internet Sources Bibliography

The following articles have been selected to supplement the diverse views presented in this chapter.

Jessica Bennett	"The Problem with Frats Isn't Just Rape. It's Power," *Time*, December 3, 2014.
Kathleen A. Bogle and Anne M. Coughlin	"The Missing Key to Fighting Sexual Assault on Campus," *Slate*, May 8, 2014.
Cherise Charleswell	"Boys Will Be Boys: America's Campus Rape Policy," Hampton Institute, July 2, 2014.
Alice Driver	"Rape Culture on Campus: The Silence of Men," Al Jazeera, December 4, 2014.
Vanessa Grigoriadis	"Meet the College Women Who Are Starting a Revolution Against Campus Sexual Assault," *New York Magazine*, September 21, 2014.
Heather Mac Donald	"The Culture of Campus 'Rape Culture,'" *National Review Online*, October 11, 2014.
Anna North	"Is College Sexual Assault a Fraternity Problem?," *New York Times*, January 29, 2015.
Abby Ohlheiser	"Study Finds 'Epidemic' of Sexual Assault Among First-Year Women at One U.S. College," *Washington Post*, May 20, 2015.
Dante Ricci	"The Prevalence of Sexual Assault on College Campuses Is Too High to Ignore," *Huffington Post*, April 22, 2015.
Christina Hoff Sommers	"Rape Culture Is a 'Panic Where Paranoia, Censorship, and False Accusations Flourish,'" *Time*, May 15, 2014.

CHAPTER 2

Are College Sexual Assault Cases Being Handled Properly?

Chapter Preface

The ongoing campus sexual assault problem is a complex, multifaceted issue that affects many people in many ways. This is particularly true with regard to the process of adjudicating individual sexual assault cases. Alleged victims, accused perpetrators, and the schools they attend all have a stake in such cases, including how they are investigated and their ultimate outcome. Because these parties' interests may often be at odds with one another, ensuring that the process for investigating and settling sexual assault cases is fair, balanced, and adequately thorough can be a difficult prospect.

As the debate over the campus sexual assault problem has unfolded, various ideas on how sexual assault cases should be handled have emerged. Some argue that these cases should be handled by law enforcement rather than college disciplinary boards. Opponents of this idea, on the other hand, suggest that colleges are actually better equipped to hear sexual assault cases—not to mention more sensitive to the needs of the parties involved—and should retain their role in the process. Some contend that colleges should make expulsion the mandatory punishment for sexual assault, while others hold that such a policy would infringe on the rights of the accused. Specific issues such as these highlight the fundamental question that underlies the entire debate over the adjudication of campus sexual assault cases: Is the process equally fair to both accusers and the accused?

For advocates on all sides of the issue, the key to effective campus sexual assault adjudication is ensuring that the interests of both parties involved are equally represented and protected throughout the process. The question of what exactly qualifies as fair in such complicated and delicate matters is anything but clear, however. Today the approach most colleges take in dealing with sexual assault cases is based on the guidelines established in Title IX, a law that is part of the United States Education Amendments of 1972, and other more recent codes put in place by the Barack Obama administration. Whether these laws are truly fair to everyone involved is hotly debated. While some think these laws offer protection to accusers and the accused and ensure that both parties have equal footing in sexual assault cases, others believe they are slanted in favor of accusers and leave the accused at an unjust disadvantage. As such, some activists argue that the system should be revamped to make it easier for accused individuals to defend themselves and avoid the undue and potentially harsh consequences of false accusations. Conversely, victims' rights advocates contend that giving accused individuals too much leverage would only serve to make it harder for accusers to get the justice they deserve and increase the chances that they will be revictimized in the process. Clearly, the way sexual assaults on campus are addressed is a contentious matter with few easy answers.

The authors of the viewpoints in the following chapter examine the fairness of the adjudication process and debate the best way to handle sexual assault cases so that justice is served as appropriately as possible to all parties involved.

> "Universities view it as their right and educational mission to create internal justice systems for their communities."

Accused College Rapists Have Rights, Too

Judith Shulevitz

In the following viewpoint, Judith Shulevitz argues that colleges' sexual assault policies are unfair to the accused. She contends that many such policies, though they do much to protect the victims of campus sexual assault, largely ignore the rights of the accused. As a result, accused individuals find themselves at the mercy of a system in which they assume virtually all of the risk and have little or no opportunity to defend themselves properly. Shulevitz is a senior science editor with the New Republic *and the author of* The Sabbath World: Glimpses of a Different Order of Time.

As you read, consider the following questions:

1. According to Shulevitz, why is it unfair to deny students accused of sexual assault direct legal representation?

2. According to Shulevitz, why are college administrators unhappy about the new sexual assault policies they are being required to develop?

3. According to Shulevitz, what can colleges do to address this situation?

This August, Columbia University released a new policy for handling "gender-based" misconduct among students. Since April, universities around the country have been rewriting their guidelines after a White House task force (http://www.whitehouse.gov/the-press-office/2014/04/29/fact-sheet-not-alone-protecting-students-sexual-assault) urged them to do more to fight sexual assault. I was curious to know what a lawyer outside the university system would make of one of these codes. So I sent the document to Robin Steinberg, a public defender and a feminist.

A few hours later, Steinberg wrote back in alarm. She had read the document with colleagues at the Bronx legal-aid center she runs. They were horrified, she said—not because Columbia still hadn't sufficiently protected survivors of assault, as some critics charge, but because its procedures revealed a cavalier disregard for the civil rights of people accused of rape, assault, and other gender-based crimes. "We are never sending our boys to college," she wrote.

Columbia's safeguards for the accused are better than most. For instance, it allows both accuser and accused to have a lawyer at a hearing, and, if asked, will locate free counsel. By contrast, Harvard, which issued a new code in July, holds investigations but not hearings and does not offer to obtain independent legal assistance. But Steinberg, like most people, hadn't realized how far the rules governing sexual conduct on campus have strayed from any commonsense understanding of justice.

Most colleges that do allow lawyers into sexual-misconduct hearings or interrogations do not permit them to speak, though they may pass notes. Students on both sides must speak for themselves. This presents a serious problem for a young man charged with rape (and in the vast majority of campus cases, the accused are men). On one hand, if he doesn't defend himself, he'll be at a disadvantage. On the other, if he is also caught up in a criminal case, anything he says in a campus procedure can be used against him in court. Neither side may cross-examine witnesses to establish contradictions in their testimony. A school may withhold the identity of an accuser from the accused if she requests anonymity (though it may choose not to). Guilt or innocence hinges on a "preponderance" of evidence, a far lower standard than the "beyond a reasonable doubt" test that prevails in courtrooms. At Harvard, the Title IX enforcement office acts as cop, prosecutor, judge, and jury—and also hears the appeals. This conflation of possibly conflicting roles is "fundamentally not due process," says Janet Halley, a Harvard Law School professor whose areas of expertise include feminist legal theory and procedural law.

How did this shadow judicial system become the norm on college campuses? Don't blame universities entirely. In 1997, the U.S. Department of Education's Office for Civil Rights (OCR) started telling colleges how to handle sexual-misconduct cases, resting its authority on Title IX, the 1972 law prohibiting discrimination on the basis of gender. (Students have always been able to file police charges.) Since then, the government has issued many guidances and revisions; Congress has passed bills. The clarification that did most to change schools' approach to misconduct was the "Dear Colleague" letter of 2011. Among other things, this document requested schools to lower their standard of proof and to conclude all proceedings swiftly, apparently without regard for the timing of any criminal investigation. If a school violates any of the many rules or recommendations, OCR may put it on the list of 84 colleges under investigation, a public-relations

Why the Rights of the Accused Matter

We need to change the culture of discourse around sexual assault on campuses. To stand up for the rights of the accused is not to attack victims or women. Our colleges, like the rest of our society, must be places where you are innocent until proven guilty. The day after graduation, young men and women will be thrown into a world where there is no Gender-Based Misconduct Office. They will have to live by the rules of society at large. Higher education should ready our students for this reality, not shield them from it.

Emily Yoffe, "The College Rape Overcorrection,"
Slate, *December 7, 2014.*

disaster. OCR could also disqualify it from receiving federal funding, which could mean shutting it down.

University officials I've talked to are upset about the policies they're being asked to write, though none would say so on the record. But Brett Sokolow, who runs a law practice that advises both universities and students, said administrators tell him they feel overwhelmed by the difficulty of handling sexual-misconduct cases and the expectation that they'll pass Solomonic judgments about complicated sexual encounters to which there may have been no witnesses and which often involve heavy drinking. OCR requires schools to train investigators as well as the panelists who hear cases, but they are rarely trained well. "We run four-day trainings for campus investigators," says Sokolow. "When these folks come out of it, if they're novices, they're not ready."

There is no question that many women who have made accusations of rape or assault have been shockingly mistreated by their schools. But since the "Dear Colleague" letter, more than 20 lawsuits have been filed against colleges by men punished for sexual misconduct, and lawyers believe there will be many more such lawsuits in the next few months. In some of these cases, the facts are too messy to be shoehorned into the master narrative of predators and victims that dominates discussions of campus sexual assault. A few reveal details about the way some schools handle people under investigation that are themselves disturbing.

A suit filed this spring against Colgate University suggests that, in their eagerness to protect the vulnerable, schools may be too quick to act on the presumption of guilt. In 2013, an ex-girlfriend accused a male undergraduate of having, a year earlier, pushed her so hard she fell. She noted that one of his former girlfriends had obtained a no-contact order against him—she too had been pushed and fell against a table, cutting her head, although the man and that woman remained friendly and she declined to join the complaint. The young man's lawsuit and Colgate's response offer very different accounts of what happened next, but the facts that Colgate does not dispute are these: Before questioning the student, Colgate had already prepared a letter of interim suspension. He didn't know this. The man was never given the option to seek counsel, even though the allegations could have led to a criminal investigation. (Colgate's reply to this assertion: "no right to counsel existed.") He was questioned for several hours, well into the night. Immediately afterward, his interrogator told him he was suspended, offered him a ticket to his home in Bangladesh, and explained that he could participate in any hearing via Skype or telephone. When the student said he didn't want to miss classes or the chance to defend himself, security officers escorted him to a room in the basement of a dorm and kept him there, under guard, for two nights. The room had neither cell reception nor Wi-Fi, so at first, he had no way to get in touch with anyone. When he asked to be released, he was told he was free to return to Bangladesh. He finally managed to contact a faculty adviser who helped him find temporary accommodation off-campus.

The student, who was expelled, is charging the school with false imprisonment, among other things. Case law on temporary student suspensions indicates he was entitled to a hearing to determine whether his was necessary; this was not offered. Whatever he did—and if true, the charges are serious—the school went outside the bounds of decency, and perhaps its own authority, by treating him as guilty before hearing his case.

A dispute at Brandeis reveals the difficulty of distinguishing between actionable abuse and relationships gone sour. According to the *Washington Post* (http://www.washingtonpost .com/local/education/behind-a-sexual-misconduct-case-at -brandeis-university-questions-on-all-sides/2014/08/20/5e2 f2160-2225-11e4-8593-da634b334390_story.html) and other reports, a gay couple dated for nearly two years, then broke up. Six months later, one ex-boyfriend accused the other of assaulting him by waking him up in the middle of the night and "aggressively" seeking sex, touching him without consent, and not giving him personal space in the bathroom. The other man said the worst he had done was kiss his boyfriend while he was sleeping. The accused was found guilty of sexual misconduct and invasion of privacy and given a disciplinary warning and ordered to complete training in sexual-assault prevention. Outraged at what he saw as an insufficient punishment, the accuser organized protests. (One featured 50 students holding signs with their mouths taped shut.) OCR is investigating whether the accused student was denied a fair hearing—possibly the first time it has taken action on behalf of the accused in this kind of case.

So what *should* colleges do about sexual assault? In February, RAINN, the Rape, Abuse, and Incest National Network,

wrote to the White House task force (https://rainn.org/news
-room/rainn-urges-white-house-task-force-to-overhaul-coll
eges-treatment-of-rape) to argue that complaints should be
dealt with by the police. Victims' rights advocates counter that
the criminal justice system is insensitive to rape victims and
bad at securing convictions. Either way, universities view it as
their right and educational mission to create internal justice
systems for their communities. The quickest fix would be to
upgrade their procedures: to ensure that the rights of both
parties are equally protected and that every administrator or
faculty member involved is properly trained. If nobody trusts
the process—and right now, nobody appears to—campus un-
rest will only grow.

What's happening at universities represents an often necessary effort to recategorize once-acceptable behaviors as unacceptable. But the government, via Title IX, is effectively acting
on the notion popularized in the 1970s and '80s by Andrea
Dworkin and Catharine MacKinnon that male domination is
so pervasive that women need special protection from the rig-
ors of the law. Men, as a class, have more power than women,
but American law rests on the principle that individuals have
rights even when accused of doing bad things. And American
liberalism has long rejected the notion that those rights may
be curtailed even for a noble cause. "We need to take into account our obligations to due process not because we are soft
on rapists and other exploiters of women," says Halley, but because "the danger of holding an innocent person responsible
is real."

> *"Equality requires that students who re-port sexual violence be regarded as equally trustworthy as the students they accuse, and that their futures be con-sidered just as bright."*

Fair Process, Not Criminal Process, Is the Right Way to Address Campus Sexual Assault

Alexandra Brodsky

In the following viewpoint, Alexandra Brodsky argues that new laws guiding how colleges are to investigate sexual assault allega-tions are fair to both the accuser and the accused. She argues that equality is paramount in such investigations and that as long as colleges completely follow through on their legal obliga-tions, both parties can expect to receive the fair treatment they deserve. Brodsky is a Yale Law School student, an editor with Feministing.com, and the cofounder of a national student cam-paign against gender-based violence called Know Your IX.

As you read, consider the following questions:

1. According to Brodsky, why is it important that we support the rights of both accusers and the accused in college sexual assault cases?

2. According to Brodsky, how does the Office for Civil Rights serve to protect students accused of sexual assault?

3. Why would it be wrong to force a college disciplinary board to adhere to a higher burden of proof in sexual assault cases, according to Brodsky?

In just a few years, the national conversation about sexual violence on college campuses has shifted from disbelief to an in-depth policy debate about how to respond to gender-based harms in the academic setting. While survivor groups push for meaningful sanctions, and universities struggle to avoid legal liability from all sides, a number of defense-minded advocates have pushed back, calling for schools to reform their internal decision making to look more like criminal adjudication. Some are defense-minded lawyers, like the 28 Harvard Law professors who published an opinion piece in the *Boston Globe*, among them Nancy Gertner, a retired federal judge I greatly admire, whose longform essay on the topic appears in the current issue of the *American Prospect* magazine. Others are "men's rights activists" who harass campus survivors on Twitter.

As an advocate for campus survivors of sexual violence, and a law student with a background in public defense, I have worried about colleges' procedural fairness for both sides, and I'm glad to see this conversation, long discussed among lawyers and activists, reach the opinion pages of mainstream publications. But the criminal law–inspired alternatives some propose are counterproductive, recreating little trials rather than responding to the unique reasons we need Title IX. They ignore that campus assaults are addressed not to vindicate the rights of the state but as part of a civil rights regime to promote gender equity in education.

Many critics, rightfully invested in protections for the accused, find this equality-driven approach hard to accept. Their discomfort—almost always focused on university decision making about rape alone, to the exclusion of other infractions—speaks to the monopoly that the criminal law holds in Americans' understanding of responses to gender-based violence. Despite the fact that U.S. civil law has long addressed these harms outside the criminal context, it is difficult to shake the feeling that rape is a matter for criminal courts alone. This narrow vision ignores both the failures of the criminal justice system, to which victims overwhelmingly choose not to report, and the diversity of harms sexual violence imposes. Rape is not only a crime. It is also a form of discrimination. That's the domain of civil, not criminal, law.

Public accounts would have you think that the interests of the two parties involved in a dispute are mutually exclusive, with advocates for victims eager for secret councils that automatically brand every accused student a rapist. That's incorrect: the interests are, instead, mutually dependent.

We recognize that the same principle that leads us to fight for students' rights to an education that is free of violence and harassment—that the opportunity to learn is central to individual dignity and social progress—also requires us to take seriously potential suspensions or expulsions of accused students. The effects of an interruption in education can be devastating, whether a student is forced off campus by a rare false allegation of rape against him or (more commonly) because she has been assaulted and doesn't feel safe staying.

Rigorous procedural protections have the additional benefit for all parties of legitimizing the systems being used, so they can't be ridiculed as "kangaroo courts," as many schools' disciplinary boards are today. Colleges will get help from students in stopping sexual violence only if their decisions about discipline are accepted by those involved and by the public. Survivors may lose faith in the system if they see it as unfair, as has happened with many crime victims who turn away from the police and criminal courts in the age of mass incarceration and documented police brutality.

The Constitution requires very few procedural protections in university decision making: The Supreme Court has found that, before a public university can impose serious permanent sanctions, the Fifth Amendment requires only that it provide notice that an offense has been alleged and that it is holding a hearing about the matter. At private institutions, the Constitution requires no procedural protections. That's not nearly enough.

The good news is that the U.S. Department of Education has recognized constitutional protections for accused students are too thin for fair and effective disciplinary systems. Through guidance to universities on how to investigate reports of sexual violence, the department's Office for Civil Rights (OCR) has not only protected survivors but also created the country's most robust regime of procedural rights for their alleged assailants. A student accused of rape, then, is provided far more protections than his classmate accused of plagiarism.

Any continued failures, then, are the fault not of the law but of schools' refusal to follow it. Just as many colleges have long ignored their duties to survivors who report violence, so are some institutions now ignoring the OCR's requirements for accused students. More robust enforcement of Title IX, then, will help students on both sides of an accusation, ensuring protection of both of their rights.

Here are procedural protections every university should provide: In accordance with OCR guidance, both accused and accusing students should be informed of their rights, decision-making boards must be informed and impartial, and they must make their decisions in a timely fashion. OCR allows both sides access to lawyers if they can afford it, but schools should go further and, to ensure equal protection regardless of financial means, offer free legal consultation and a specially trained advocate to each student, complainant and respondent. Accused students should be provided with a detailed account of the allegations against them so they can respond in an informed way. Accommodations should be made to ensure respondents also facing criminal charges are not forced to self-incriminate (though, as in civil trials, decision makers should be allowed to take non-responses into account). Each party should also be able to submit reasonable questions for the adjudicating board to ask the other side. Over time, as schools refine the systems they are building today, it will become clear that further protections are needed and what they should be.

These campus policy reforms should benefit all involved: I spent much of this fall reading through lawsuits against schools from both respondents and those making sexual assault allegations against them, and often the two sides' procedural complaints were indistinguishable.

However, some critics, like the group of Harvard professors, Koch-funded libertarian men's groups and, to a lesser extent, Gertner, want campus decision making about gender-based violence to look not like other forms of university discipline—which deal with offenses ranging from plagiarism to drug sales in dorms—but more like the criminal justice system. These critics call for gender-violence school proceedings run more like trials than today's campus investigations, which sometimes never see both parties in a room together. Rather than private interviews, these critics imagine combative hearings with lawyers, or even the accused students themselves, cross-examining the alleged victims and decision makers imposing near criminal-level evidentiary burdens.

But school investigations don't look like trials because they aren't supposed to. Procedural protections run along a sliding scale in American law: The more serious the stakes, the harder we make it to prove a case. For example, civil courts—which can impose fines (and resulting reputational harms) but cannot levy prison sentences—provide fewer procedural protections than criminal courts. Like a civil verdict, an expulsion may be devastating, but does not compare in severity to incarceration. So it makes sense that the American system of justice makes it harder to get a conviction by a criminal jury than a finding of culpability by a university.

And, crucially, where the criminal law seeks to punish, Title IX (the 1972 federal civil rights statute that forbids sex discrimination in education) seeks to engender equality. Schools are required to respond to gender-based violence as part of a broad obligation to promote equality. Title IX demands we value the education of women students (who are more likely to be victimized) just as much as that of their male peers (who are more likely to be victimizers). In a university proceeding under the statute, as in a civil rights trial and not a criminal trial, the victim is a full party to the proceeding and his or her interests are considered just as important as the accused's.

That's why, for example, all civil law responses to gender-based violence use the "preponderance of the evidence" standard for what must be proved by the complaining party. This evidentiary burden is required by sexual harassment and violence lawsuits under civil rights and tort law; federal agency processing of Title VII claims of harassment and violence in the workplace; prison decision making under the Prison Rape Elimination Act; and, as required by the Department of Education, university disciplinary investigations.

The department's policy guidance reflects decades of civil law precedent, from a wide range of adjudicators and contexts, about how best to balance the interest in promoting gender equality against the interest in avoiding false findings of responsibility. A preponderance means more than half, so if most of the evidence suggests responsibility, or a lack of it, that's the conclusion the board should make. To do otherwise—to find, for example, that most of the evidence suggests a student raped a classmate, but to find him or her not responsible nonetheless because the decision-making process requires a higher burden of proof—is to value one student's education over the other's.

Gertner worries that other aspects of campus decision making, compared with a civil trial, are so deficient that the standard requirement for evidence is too low. I agree with the professor that certain campus policies, like entirely excluding lawyers from the process, might stymy a search for truth. But the solution is not to place a bigger evidentiary burden on the alleged victim. Rather, we should solve the problem at its root. And, for *rightful* deviations from the trial-model, there is no need to so "compensate."

The equality principles underlying university decision making also require that a school must take into account an interest criminal courts do not: the victim's physical and psychological safety during the hearing process. Unlike universities, which respond to sexual violence under a broad mandate of combating gender-based discrimination and hostility, the state prosecutes these crimes to vindicate its *own* rights, with little regard for the survivor's desires or feelings. Some proposed school reforms modeled on criminal practice, like providing accused students (or their lawyers in their presence) the chance to directly question their alleged victim, likely would contribute to the kind of hostile environment that these proceedings are supposed to remediate. Schools have a responsibility to make sure that victims don't need to live or study or even speak with their assailants. Their investigations should not create the very situations they were charged to prevent, nor dissuade survivors from coming forward.

Schools, then, should continue to innovate, trying solutions that balance these interests like asking accused students to provide written questions to later be asked of the complainant by the board. They can also allow complaining students to answer directed questions in a written statement, analogous to written depositions outlined in the Federal Rules of Civil Procedure.

Some critics, I believe, are so focused on the criminal justice system in their professional and academic lives that they fail to appreciate in full the different goals and consequences of campus disciplinary hearings. I also worry that, for some but not all, this devotion to the criminal law response suggests a subtle misogyny that many focusing on this issue have internalized. No one cries foul when a student is expelled for cheating on an exam based on the preponderance of the evidence. Yet many mourn the lost "bright futures" of classmates accused of rape. And they insist that accusations of gender-based violence, and only gender-based violence, be put to the test of the criminal justice system. In doing so, they invoke old, insidious myths about the woman who "cries rape," found everywhere from the Bible to the Model Penal Code. Why do we think an accusation of sexual assault is any more likely to be false than an accusation of a punch in the face? The answer necessarily lies in the differing confidence placed in different kinds of victims—and there is a special skepticism reserved for anyone who claims to have been raped.

Virtually everyone supports equality in education for men and women, as required by Title IX. But that equality requires placing survivors and their assailants on a level field—which current campus procedures try to do and criminal law–inspired proposals would not. Equality requires that students who report sexual violence be regarded as equally trustworthy as the students they accuse, and that their futures be considered just as bright.

> *"If assailants on campus know that a police investigation awaits, and not a campus 'process,' I am willing to bet it gets their attention."*

Campus Sexual Assault Cases Should Be Handled by Police

David M. Rubin

In the following viewpoint, David M. Rubin argues that colleges should leave the investigation of sexual assault cases to the police rather than adjudicating these matters internally. He contends that college justice systems are woefully inadequate when it comes to doling out justice in sexual assault cases and should, therefore, defer to authorities that are better equipped to handle such sensitive and complex complaints. He also adds that doing so will help to relieve colleges of the heavy financial burden related to the investigation of sexual assault claims. Formerly the dean of the S.I. Newhouse School of Public Communications at Syracuse University, Rubin is a columnist whose work has appeared in the Syracuse Post-Standard.

As you read, consider the following questions:

1. According to Rubin, what was the Barack Obama administration seeking to accomplish by releasing the list of schools under investigation for how they handled sexual assault complaints?

2. Why does Rubin doubt colleges' ability to adjudicate sexual assault cases themselves?

3. According to Rubin, what should colleges specifically do instead of investigating sexual assaults themselves?

When I was an undergraduate at Columbia University in the 1960s, we had neither female students nor coed dorms. If we invited a woman to our room during limited visiting hours, the door had to remain open, and we each had to keep one foot on the floor to prevent a sudden outbreak of moofky-poofky. The dorms at Barnard [College], the women's college across the street, were forbidden territory.

It seems not to have occurred to administrators at Columbia that cheap hotel rooms, cars, and frat houses could substitute for monastic dorm rooms. My recollection is that they didn't much care.

They care now. The [Barack] Obama administration has recently declared war on campus sexual violence and has put college administrators on the hot seat.

The Obama Administration vs. Campus Sexual Violence

In late April [2014] the administration released a 20-page report from the [White House] Task Force to Protect Students from Sexual Assault. The report pointedly reminded campus administrators that they "are obliged to protect students from sexual assault" if they want to receive federal funds.

On May 1 the Department of Education upped the ante by releasing the names of 55 schools under investigation for how they have handled sexual assault complaints. These schools have not been found guilty of anything. Rather, students complained to the department that their campus administrators ignored them or bungled the investigations, thereby doubly victimizing them.

The unusual release of this list made the Obama administration's intentions clear: College officials must take this problem seriously if they want the mother's milk of federal money. The administration wants to see a federally approved process in place that will provide alleged victims with a hearing and a satisfactory resolution.

Young women and men not fortunate enough to be in college are, of course, frequently the victims of sexual assault in our towns and cities, but the president did not address that. Colleges are the more attractive political target.

So another amped-up federal mandate has landed on the desks of college presidents. Creating a "process" for dealing fairly and expeditiously with sexual assault allegations will require a campus bureaucracy to write rules, hear cases, adjudicate them, hand out penalties, and enforce them—all the while providing due process and equal protection rights to all parties (including the alleged perpetrator).

This will cost colleges money. Yet just a few months ago, the Obama administration called on higher education to address the problem of exploding costs. It threatened to set up a system to rate the economic value of colleges in order to force down costs, a half-baked idea to begin with that has so far gone nowhere. Now comes this. Does the left hand of this administration know what the right hand is doing?

The Problem with College Justice Systems

One reason for the astronomical cost of higher education is the elaborate campus safety net of services that students, parents and the government already demand. These programs

Law Enforcement Gets Sexual Assault Cases Right

There's no question that the real police frequently treat rape charges with undue doubtfulness and callousness. But it's not clear that universities do better—and they frequently do even worse. At the very least, police have the tools to treat rape like the crime that it is and accused rapists like the criminals that they may be.

Mark Joseph Stern,
"Colleges Aren't Equipped to Investigate Rape,"
Slate, *February 24, 2015.*

may be useful to some students, but they do not directly improve the classroom experience that, I thought, was the point of a college education.

So it's time to ask the fundamental question: Are educators capable of adjudicating sexual assault cases, and should the Obama administration even ask them to try?

I have served as a judge on academic integrity cases at SU [Syracuse University]—cheating, plagiarism, and the like. I have witnessed some bizarre outcomes in which justice was not done for either the student or the faculty member.

So why should we expect panels of faculty, staff and students to handle infinitely more difficult, highly charged cases of sexual assault that may involve alcohol, drugs, unconsciousness, miscommunication about consent, remorse, guilt, and more? This is best left to police specialists trained for this work. Sexual assault is a crime. We would not expect a university to adjudicate an armed robbery on campus through its own parallel "justice" system, so why should it adjudicate sexual assault? Indeed, why should a university even *have* its own parallel justice system?

A Better Alternative

It would be less expensive and more effective for a college to designate one of its own as the point person for sexual assault complaints. That person would be the liaison to local police. She or he would follow the case through to its conclusion to assure the rights of *both* parties were safeguarded.

Taking on these cases will cost local police departments money. Given that colleges are tax-exempt entities, taxpayers may not want to foot this extra bill. So the colleges should pay a fee for this service.

This approach will be cheaper and more likely to produce an outcome that does not violate the constitutional rights of either party. As an added bonus, if sexual predators on campus know that the starting point is a police station, and not an on-campus, never-ending, easily-manipulated "process," it would be a real deterrent.

If assailants on campus know that a police investigation awaits, and not a campus "process," I am willing to bet it gets their attention.

> "Because schools have a national man-
> date to provide a safe and equitable
> learning environment, they are in a
> unique position to best adjudicate cam-
> pus rapes."

Campus Sexual Assault Cases Should Be Handled by School Officials

Caroline Heldman and Baillee Brown

In the following viewpoint, Caroline Heldman and Baillee Brown argue that campus sexual assault cases should be adjudicated by college authorities and not by law enforcement. They assert that colleges are better equipped for such matters and that difficult experiences with the police tend to be re-traumatizing for survivors. For these reasons, they believe that continuing to allow colleges to investigate sexual assault cases will lead to better outcomes for everyone involved. Heldman is an Occidental College associate professor of politics and an anti-rape activist. Brown, at the time of writing, was a politics major studying at Occidental College.

As you read, consider the following questions:

1. According to Heldman and Brown, why does experiencing the trauma of sexual assault sometimes make victims seem less believable to law enforcement?

2. Why should sexual assault survivors avoid going to the police, according to campus rape survivor Emma Sulkowicz?

3. According to Heldman and Brown, why are colleges particularly well suited for adjudicating sexual assault cases?

There's one question about campus rape that comes up again and again: Why isn't the crime handled exclusively by law enforcement? In a perfect world, the legal system would effectively arbitrate this crime, but given law enforcement's dismal record on sex crimes, schools have no choice but to adjudicate campus rapes in order to comply with federal Title IX law.

Police Shortcomings

Law enforcement is not a viable solution to campus rape because police do a terrible job of holding rapists accountable. According to a recent analysis of Department of Justice data, only 3 percent of *all* rapists—not just campus rapists—will ever spend a day in jail. Only 40 percent of all rapes are reported to police, and of those, only 10 percent will lead to a felony conviction with slightly fewer seeing the inside of a jail cell.

The numbers are no better when it comes to law enforcement's handling of campus sex crimes. In 2011, the *Chicago Tribune* published the results of a study involving 171 campus sex complaints at six Midwestern universities. Twelve of the accused perpetrators were arrested, and only four were convicted. The *Tribune* concludes that such low arrest (7 percent) and conviction (2.3 percent) rates leave "untold numbers of college women feeling betrayed and vulnerable, believing that their allegations are not taken seriously."

Law enforcement is hampered in prosecuting rape because this crime is rarely witnessed by a third party. Plus, physical evidence may look similar to consensual sex, the standard of reasonable doubt is high (approximately 95 percent certainty) and, in most states, the burden of proof is on the survivor to prove s/he was raped instead of the defendant proving that s/he obtained consent.

Additionally, trauma impairs the prefrontal cortex, which is crucial to decision making and memory, so survivors may come off as less believable to authorities when they report the crime. Survivors often recount their rapes with little emotion and are unable to remember details or give a linear account of events due to impaired brain functioning.

Furthermore, widely held rape myths work against reporting, arrest, and conviction rates for rape, including the myth that only "stranger rape" and interactions that result in physical damage constitute "real" rape. Prosecutors have broad discretion in whether to prosecute a case or not, and they tend to be more concerned about their win-loss record than pursuing justice in cases that are difficult to win.

Traumatic Experiences

One of this [viewpoint's] authors, Caroline, has worked with more than a dozen campus survivors who have reported rapes to police in recent years. Not a single case resulted in an arrest, and in addition to being a waste of time, the experience often re-traumatized the survivors. A district attorney in California closed USC [University of Southern California] student Tucker Reed's case without taking an official statement from her, despite the fact that she had a recorded conversation with her alleged perpetrator apologizing for raping her.

When Morgan Carpenter filed a rape claim in New York, an assistant district attorney told her, "Well, I met him. He's

Colleges Are Better Equipped to Handle Sexual Assault Cases

The history of Title IX illuminates a fact that is too often overlooked in conversations about campus rape today: University adjudication is neither a substitute for nor a direct parallel to the criminal justice system. After all, student-victims can report to both their universities and the police; the two systems are not mutually exclusive. Campus adjudication is a separate antidiscrimination right protecting students' access to educational opportunities at their schools, unburdened by historical and persistent gender-based disparities.

Alexandra Brodsky and Elizabeth Deutsch,
"No, We Can't Just Leave College Sexual Assault to the Police,"
Politico, *December 3, 2014.*

really cute. Maybe you just had a weak moment and you thought maybe you could get away with it."

Caroline worked with a survivor who was raped in Michigan in the spring of 2013. She awoke in the middle of a rape in a fraternity house, kicked off her assailant, ran into the street half clothed and called the police. Her rape kit indicated serious physical damage that would not heal for two weeks. The DA [district attorney] refused to press charges, citing a lack of physical evidence.

A recent college graduate in Florida who was raped in the spring of 2014 in her off-campus apartment went straight to the police to report her rape and was told there "was nothing" they could do about it. She then documented the rape through a series of text messages and a recorded conversation in which the alleged perpetrator admitted holding her down, forcing her to have sex, and seeing the "pain on your face." The DA refused to move the case forward due to a lack of witnesses and physical evidence, and even accused the survivor of "flirting" with the alleged perpetrator by contacting him to obtain his admission of the crime—as she was instructed to do by the police.

After her experience with the police, Columbia University student survivor Emma Sulkowicz said she would discourage other survivors from reporting to law enforcement:

> *If you want to go to the police, this is what to expect: You'll be verbally abused. But at least no one will yell at you for not going to the police and getting verbally abused. Just take your pick.*

Why Schools Are Better Suited for Adjudicating Sexual Assault

Most schools do a poor job processing sexual assault/rape cases, but the criminal justice system is even worse. In the absence of a viable law enforcement option, schools have to conduct their own investigations and adjudications to be in compliance with federal law. These adjudication processes vary from campus to campus, but they are invariably less formal than a legal investigation.

But schools are uniquely positioned to identify and sanction rapists since the Department of Education has mandated the "preponderance of evidence" standard, the same standard of proof used in civil cases. Some have criticized this standard, but campus rape adjudications are not criminal proceedings, and the stiffest sanction (expulsion) is a rarely used slap on the wrist compared to a felony conviction. Rape on campus is currently treated as harshly as plagiarism. Additionally, perpetrators who are expelled are able to transfer with relative ease, both before and after they are sanctioned, because schools do not report rape as the reason for expulsion on student transcripts. (This is why we need a national database of campus rapists so schools can keep their student body safe by not accepting rapists from other campuses.)

Law enforcement is a terrible option for campus rape survivors because it is ineffective and often re-traumatizing for survivors. But because schools have a national mandate to provide a safe and equitable learning environment, they are in a unique position to best adjudicate campus rapes. Therefore it is incumbent on them to establish fair, effective, and transparent reporting, investigation, adjudication and sanctioning processes that reflect best practices. It is also incumbent on administrators to work with local law enforcement to improve the way both institutions respond to this heinous crime.

> "Instead of contriving methods to prevent people from being assaulted, we should focus on deterring that kind of behavior altogether by making expulsion the default consequence for those found guilty of severe types of sexual violence."

Students Who Commit Sexual Assaults Should Be Subject to Mandatory Expulsion

Kinjo Kiema

In the following viewpoint, Kinjo Kiema argues that expulsion should be the mandatory punishment for students found guilty of sexual assault. She contends that mandatory expulsion would be a stronger deterrent than other, lighter punishments and would serve not only to help survivors feel more comfortable on campus after being assaulted but also to prevent sexual assaults from happening in the first place. At the time of writing, Kiema was a political communication and American studies student at George Washington University.

As you read, consider the following questions:

1. According to Kiema, why is the idea of mandatory expulsion not actually as severe as it sounds?

2. In Kiema's view, what is wrong with Dartmouth's mandatory expulsion policy, and how can it be improved?

3. According to Kiema, why are sexual assault survivors often reluctant to report the abuse they have suffered?

We've heard all the suggestions countless times—don't walk alone at night, never accept an open drink, carry pepper spray with you, don't wear clothes that are too suggestive, don't drink too much.

Universally, these recommendations imply the same thing: Women, please alter your behavior to avoid unwanted and unwarranted violence against yourself. It's nothing innovative or progressive to tell women that the solution to sexual violence lies within. (Besides, let's remember that even if I were to avoid alcohol consumption in social situations, it wouldn't stop a potential predator from assaulting someone else.)

Last week [in February 2015], student leaders floated a proposal to incorporate mandatory sexual violence training into Colonial Inauguration [a student orientation program at George Washington (GW) University]. Teaching new students—especially those leaving home for the first time—about sexual violence and bystander intervention is a wonderful place to start.

Going Further

But GW could and should do more. Instead of contriving methods to prevent people from being assaulted, we should focus on deterring that kind of behavior altogether by making expulsion the default consequence for those found guilty of severe types of sexual violence.

Expulsion isn't the default punishment at most universities. In fact, just one so far—Dartmouth College—has made it

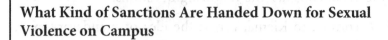

What Kind of Sanctions Are Handed Down for Sexual Violence on Campus

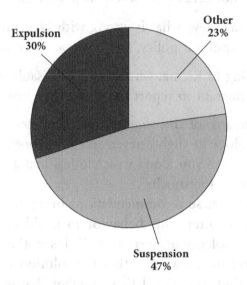

Other
23%

Expulsion
30%

Suspension
47%

TAKEN FROM: Tyler Kingkade, "Fewer than One-Third of Campus Sexual Assault Cases Result in Expulsion," *Huffington Post*, September 29, 2014.

mandatory, while some others—including Duke and Stanford Universities—have adjusted their policies to make it the "preferred" sanction. But GW could be one of the schools leading the way in combating the epidemic of sexual violence on campuses by adopting mandatory expulsion.

This policy would guarantee that students who are found guilty of violent and criminal acts would never be allowed back at our university. Without it, we jeopardize the safety of students here, and force survivors to potentially have to interact with their attackers.

Although it sounds extreme, this isn't really a radical idea when you think about it. There are plenty of other serious rule violations that will cause you to be removed from campus permanently, like repeated drug violations or academic dishonesty.

As it stands, the consequences for sexual violence are—at minimum—a year of suspension and eviction from university-owned housing. That's problematic because if the minimum is applied, perpetrators are essentially just getting a couple semesters off before they return to GW.

Of course, "Every case is decided on its own facts, including when a violation is found and what the severity of the sanction will be," university spokesman Kurt Hiatt told me. But Hiatt declined to detail how often the minimum consequences are applied and how often students are expelled.

Moving Toward Mandatory Expulsion

Other schools are already heading toward adopting mandatory expulsion policies, with the goal of both protecting survivors and sending the message that sexual assault is inexcusable.

Last summer, Dartmouth made expulsion the mandatory consequence for those found guilty of "extreme cases" of sexual assault, though it failed to define "extreme cases" clearly—or at all. Defining what constitutes "extreme," and then ensuring that those found guilty are permanently removed from campus, would prevent the policy from being arbitrarily applied.

Similarly, Duke made expulsion the "preferred sanction" for those found guilty of sexual assault, and students at Stanford advocated for the policy change after campus-wide protests.

Dartmouth is one of 94 schools under investigation for Title IX violations—while Duke, Stanford and GW are not. So, clearly, schools are mobilizing to adjust their policies even without the motivation of having spots on their records.

Challenges and Opportunities

Still, some have argued that mandatory expulsion will lead to fewer people reporting incidents of sexual violence because if the perpetrator is someone a survivor knows, [the survivor] will hesitate to have [the perpetrator] kicked off campus permanently. That's a problem created by the fact that almost all survivors know their assailants—might share a friend group, even—and would fear social repercussions.

But survivors can also be deterred because they think they'll be forced to go through a grueling process and the university will still take little to no action. In the recent campus-wide sexual violence survey, half of students said they "didn't know" whether the university would respond helpfully to a reported incident, showing a widespread lack of trust in the school's ability to tackle the issue appropriately. For these survivors, it's essential they know that if their assailant is found guilty, they'll be removed from campus immediately.

Reporting of sexual violence is rare in general. The higher rate of reporting at GW this year shows that more people feel comfortable seeking help from authorities after an abuse. However, on a campus of 10,000 students, where 36 percent of female upperclassmen and 35 percent of LGBT [lesbian, gay, bisexual, and transgender] students said they had experienced "unwanted sexual behavior," there is clearly more work to do.

It might be challenging for us to accept, but eradicating sexual assault on campus can only be accomplished by grasping the problem at the root: targeting those who perpetuate this culture of violence.

> *"If Stanford adopts a harsher penalty of mandatory expulsion, then it must strongly consider raising the standard of proof and prohibiting accusers from pursuing an appeal if the initial [alternate review process] . . . does not yield a favorable outcome."*

Mandatory Expulsion for Sexual Assault Could Be an Inappropriate Response

Brandon Camhi

In the following viewpoint, Brandon Camhi argues that mandatory expulsion is not an acceptable form of punishment for campus sexual assaults given the current approach to adjudicating these cases. Specifically, he contends that since collegiate systems for trying sexual assault cases, such as Stanford University's alternate review process (ARP), do not adequately protect the rights of the accused, any mandatory expulsion policy would potentially be unfair to defendants. At the time of writing, Camhi was a Stanford economics major and the editor in chief of the Stanford Review.

As you read, consider the following questions:

1. According to Camhi, in what way is the design of the ARP board inherently unfair to the accused?

2. According to Camhi, what is the relationship between the standard of proof in ARP sexual assault hearings and the fairness of mandatory expulsion?

3. According to Camhi, how does the ARP violate the Fifth Amendment rights of the accused?

On Thursday June 5th [2014], hundreds of students gathered in White Plaza to protest Stanford's sexual assault response policies. The rally was spawned by an email from Leah Francis (Class '14) that detailed her experience navigating Stanford's alternate review process (ARP). Francis called for "mandatory expulsion for individuals found guilty of sexual assault." Francis's experience is heartbreaking and unsettling. Rapists should be punished severely, and expulsion should definitely be seriously considered. However, for mandatory expulsion to be implemented, the ARP must be reformed to better protect the rights of the accused. In its current form, the ARP does not adequately ensure that defendants receive a fair hearing.

How Campus Sexual Assaults Are Tried

First, it is important to understand how the ARP review board is selected. Five members, three of which are students and two of which are faculty, review and decide the case. Students should undoubtedly be the triers of fact in the case, because the concept of a jury of peers is an essential bedrock of our legal system. However, unlike the American judicial system, the trier of fact (the review panel) also decides procedural and evidentiary questions. For example, the accused student is allowed to submit questions for the review board to ask opposing witnesses. The review panel has the power to decide whether the questions are germane to the case. The panel can refuse to ask the accused's questions if they are "unduly incendiary" or if the information "has no bearing on a finding." In a normal criminal trial, the judge rules on objections over questions, and they are usually argued outside the presence of the jury. This prevents the jury from being prejudiced by improper questions. By merging the judge and jury, the ARP removes this critical protection. This protection is especially important given traditional methods of cross-examination are removed from the ARP review process.

Second, the ARP uses a "preponderance of the evidence" as its standard of proof which it defines as "more likely than not" that an assault occurred. This standard is used in most civil cases in the United States. In a society that claims to prefer having the guilty walk free instead of the innocent wrongfully convicted, it is troubling that many advocate the harsh penalty of mandatory expulsion given the low legal standard of proof. Surviving a sexual assault is undoubtedly an extremely traumatizing experience, but mandatory expulsion coupled with a low standard of proof makes it too easy to ruin potentially innocent students' futures. Although Stanford's judicial system is different from America's and it can choose whichever standard it wishes to determine university punishments, it is important to consider that a preponderance of the evidence was considered too low an evidentiary standard in the United States because it does not do enough to protect the accused.

Before Stanford considers mandatory expulsion, it must raise the standard of proof to either "clear and convincing evidence" or "beyond a reasonable doubt." The latter is the standard for most criminal cases in America, and it is the highest level of proof. Since Stanford does not administer criminal penalties, a "clear and convincing evidence" standard that requires that "a party must prove that it is substantially more likely than not that it is true" will adequately protect the accused and still ensure justice. It strikes a better balance than the current "preponderance of the evidence" standard of proof.

Finally, the ARP fails to defend the accused against double jeopardy, which is being tried more than once for the same crime. The ARP gives the vice provost for student affairs the power to assess on appeal whether "given the proper facts, criteria and procedures, was the reviewers' decision reasonable?" This offers broad latitude for a reversal of an acquittal, especially given the low standard of proof the accuser must meet. Like the standard of proof, Stanford is free to allow double jeopardy since it is separate from the American judicial system. Nevertheless, it is useful to understand why the Constitution protects Americans from double jeopardy.

Sexual Assault, Punishments, and the Law

The Fifth Amendment of the U.S. Constitution defends citizens against double jeopardy. The double jeopardy clause "guarantees that the state cannot ignore the outcome of a trial and start a new one just because it does not like the outcome of the first trial." In [an] era where universities are under intense pressure from the federal government to crack down on sexual assault, a protection from double jeopardy would be a powerful defense for accused students, yet the ARP does not offer this protection.

It is an outrage that Francis's assailant was not punished more harshly. However, in our fury, we must not cast aside the rule of law and protections against the accused. If Stanford adopts a harsher penalty of mandatory expulsion, then it must strongly consider raising the standard of proof and prohibiting accusers from pursuing an appeal if the initial ARP decision process does not yield a favorable outcome.

Periodical and Internet Sources Bibliography

The following articles have been selected to supplement the diverse views presented in this chapter.

| Abigail Bessler | "Universities Keep Failing to Actually Punish Rapists," *ThinkProgress*, June 13, 2014. |

| Frank Daniels III | "Campus Sex Assaults Should Be Handled by Police," *Tennessean* (Nashville), February 21, 2015. |

| Miles Inserra | "Rights of Students Accused of Assault Often Overlooked," *Orion* (California State University, Chico), February 25, 2015. |

| Caroline Kitchener | "Two Ways to Fix How Colleges Respond to Sexual Assault," *Atlantic*, January 29, 2014. |

| Jed Rubenfeld | "Mishandling Rape," *New York Times*, November 15, 2014. |

| Tovia Smith | "Some Accused of Sexual Assault on Campus Say System Works Against Them," NPR, September 3, 2014. |

| Mark Joseph Stern | "Colleges Aren't Equipped to Investigate Rape," *Slate*, February 24, 2015. |

| Valerie Strauss | "Why Sexual Assault Cases on Campus Are Often Investigated by School, Not Police," *Washington Post*, May 2, 2014. |

| Teresa Watanabe | "College Administrators Learning to Be Sexual Misconduct Detectives," *Los Angeles Times*, May 14, 2014. |

| Emily Yoffe | "The College Rape Overcorrection," *Slate*, December 7, 2014. |

CHAPTER 3

How Might the College Sexual Assault Problem Be Addressed?

Chapter Preface

Overcoming the problem of campus sexual assault is anything but a simple, straightforward task. In itself, sexual assault is a complex issue with no clear-cut causes or obvious solutions. Furthermore, most approaches to addressing the problem have inherent risks that have to be carefully weighed and balanced to determine whether they are truly worth pursuing. Even then, few methods are likely to receive universal support from people on all sides of the debate. Clearly, no easy answers exist.

Fortunately, however, the difficulties of developing methods for addressing the campus sexual assault problem have not dissuaded enterprising, dedicated people from seeking out new opportunities. Over time, numerous methods for combating campus sexual assault have been suggested and even employed. One of the most talked-about approaches is allowing sororities to host their own parties, which would offer college women a safer alternative to the notoriously dangerous parties traditionally held only at fraternities. Another hotly debated suggestion is to relax weapons restrictions and allow students to carry guns on campus for self-defense purposes.

One modern, innovative approach to the campus sexual assault problem that is currently gaining traction is the use of sexual assault–related smartphone applications. In recent years, several apps have hit the market and have found users on college campuses across America. Some apps, such as Circle of 6, aim to prevent sexual assaults by providing users with direct and discreet access to a network of friends who can get them out of potentially dangerous situations before an incident occurs. Others, such as Callisto, provide sexual assault survivors a means of easily recording the details of their ordeal and reporting it to the proper authorities with minimal risk of retraumatization.

Some commenters have lauded these apps as important breakthroughs that are revolutionizing the fight against campus sexual assault, empowering victims, and helping to prevent others from becoming victims. Critics, however, argue that apps such as Circle of 6 and Callisto fall short of expectations, mostly because, while helpful, they fail to address the broader cultural problems from which the campus sexual assault problem stems. Critics also cite the fact that the availability of these apps is naturally limited to people who can afford to own expensive smartphones, leaving many people who are most at risk of sexual assault without access to them.

Regardless of whether sexual assault apps are or are not a good method of addressing the problem, it is hard to argue that any means of combating the campus sexual assault problem is at least worth investigating. The viewpoints in the following chapter examine some of the ways in which sexual assault on campus may be addressed.

> *"Allowing law-abiding citizens to carry guns on campus . . . would unquestionably help to prevent some rapes and additional sexual assaults on campus."*

Expanded On-Campus Gun Rights Would Reduce Sexual Assaults

Adam B. Summers

In the following viewpoint, Adam B. Summers argues that allowing students to carry firearms on campus would be an effective way to combat the college sexual assault problem. He contends that the gun-free zones established on many college campuses leave students vulnerable to attack and unable to defend themselves from sexual aggressors. If students were allowed to arm themselves, he believes, fewer sexual assaults would occur. Summers is a San Diego–based writer and public policy consultant.

As you read, consider the following questions:

1. According to Summers, why are liberals reluctant to embrace less restrictive gun laws as a way to fight the campus sexual assault problem?

2. How many defensive gun uses occur in the United States every year, according to Summers?

3. According to Summers, how was student Amanda Collins harmed by the regulations regarding guns on her college campus?

In state legislatures across the nation, lawmakers are addressing an interesting confluence of issues: sexual violence on college campuses and gun rights. President Barack Obama and many on the left have called for public and private actions to address sexual assaults on campus, and gun rights advocates, who tend to hail more from the right, have seized on the issue by touting the ability of armed self-defense to prevent and deter attacks—in the absence of campus "gun-free zones," that is.

The *New York Times* reports that legislators are considering bills that would allow the carrying of firearms on college campuses in 10 states: Florida, Indiana, Montana, Nevada, Oklahoma, South Carolina, South Dakota, Tennessee, Texas and Wyoming. Nine states currently permit campus carry.

In September, the Obama administration launched the "It's On Us" awareness campaign to attempt to reduce instances of sexual violence on campus. "It is on all of us to reject the quiet tolerance of sexual assault and to refuse to accept what's unacceptable," Obama said.

Except, it seems, when a partial solution to the problem conflicts with other liberal sensibilities.

The Benefits of Gun Freedom

There is no denying that guns are commonly used to prevent crimes and save lives. Numerous studies have estimated that there are anywhere from 800,000 to 2.5 million defensive gun

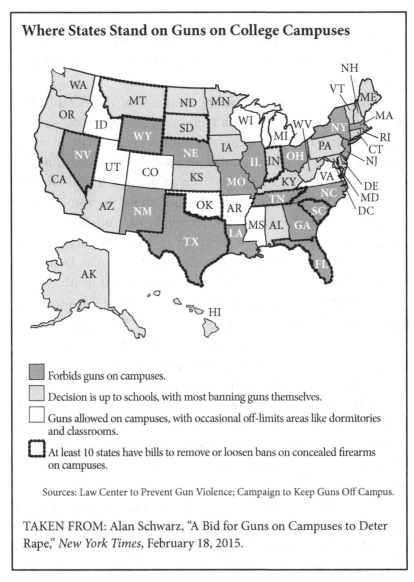

Where States Stand on Guns on College Campuses

Forbids guns on campuses.

Decision is up to schools, with most banning guns themselves.

Guns allowed on campuses, with occasional off-limits areas like dormitories and classrooms.

At least 10 states have bills to remove or loosen bans on concealed firearms on campuses.

Sources: Law Center to Prevent Gun Violence; Campaign to Keep Guns Off Campus.

TAKEN FROM: Alan Schwarz, "A Bid for Guns on Campuses to Deter Rape," *New York Times*, February 18, 2015.

uses every year in the United States. According to a widely cited study by Gary Kleck, a criminology professor at Florida State University, there are 2.2 million to 2.5 million defensive gun uses annually. A sample of those cases revealed that 8.2 percent were defenses against attempted rape and sexual assault, and 30.4 percent were defenses against other types of assault.

Establishing gun-free zones, on campus or elsewhere, only guarantees that the people in these zones will be defenseless against an attacker willing to disobey the law, no matter how strict it is.

Some of the most compelling evidence of this is embodied in the experience of Amanda Collins, a University of Nevada, Reno, student raped in a campus parking garage late at night. Ms. Collins owned a concealed weapon permit, but dutifully obeyed the law preventing her from bringing her gun on campus. Her attacker, James Biela, did not show the same fidelity to the law when he put a gun to her head, pulled her to the asphalt and raped her. He went on to rape another woman, then to rape and murder another student, Brianna Dennison, before being caught, convicted and sentenced to death.

Ms. Collins has since testified on behalf of campus carry bills in Nevada and other states. "On Oct. 22, 2007, my right to say 'No' was taken away from me by both James Biela and the Nevada legislation that has decided there should be an arbitrary line where university campuses begin," she affirmed in powerful and heartbreaking testimony before the Nevada Assembly Judiciary Committee on one such bill in 2013. "The choice to participate in one's defense should be left to the individual. That individual choice should not be mandated by the government."

She, additionally, related how she was haunted by the thought about how things might have turned out differently if she had had her gun that night. "At some point, I would have been able to stop my attack while it was in progress, and, consequently, two other known rapes would have been prevented, and a young life would have been saved," she maintained.

Allowing law-abiding citizens to carry guns on campus, or in other places designated gun-free zones, would unquestionably help to prevent some rapes and additional sexual assaults on campus, just as it prevents these and many other crimes in other public places or at home. If people have gone through the background checks and training necessary to obtain a concealed carry permit, why shouldn't they be allowed to exercise their right on campus? And how can those on the left say "No" to a measure that will advance their goal of reducing sexual violence on college campuses?

> *"Sexual assault and rape are violent crimes that might only turn more violent in the long run when guns are involved."*

Expanded On-Campus Gun Rights Would Not Reduce Sexual Assaults

Lauren Barbato

In the following viewpoint, Lauren Barbato argues that allowing students to carry guns on campus will not help to curb the ongoing sexual assault problem. Rather, she asserts that such a move would only serve to increase the likelihood of domestic violence incidents. Further, she contends that supporters of relaxed campus gun policies intentionally misrepresent how most campus sexual assaults happen so as to bolster support for their cause. Barbato is a writer who specializes in topics such as reproductive rights, politics, and religion. Her work has appeared on news websites and in magazines such as Bustle *and* Ms.

As you read, consider the following questions:

1. According to Barbato, what should be done to combat sexual assault instead of encouraging women to arm themselves?

2. In Barbato's view, what do pro-gun activists get wrong about how most campus sexual assaults happen?

3. According to the *American Journal of Public Health* study Barbato cites, what percentage of women who experienced domestic violence were able to successfully use a handgun in self-defense?

Conservative lawmakers from Florida to Nevada have found the solution to ending sexual assault on college campuses: guns. The *New York Times* reports that legislators in 10 states are currently pushing for college students to carry firearms on campuses, in a move to purportedly protect female students from sexual violence. At odds with this new gun-toting movement, however, is the long-held theory that guns may make young women more susceptible to sexual and physical violence.

Allowing Guns on Campus

Concealed carry of firearms is currently banned on college grounds in 20 states, while another 23 states have laws leaving the decision to ban concealed firearms up to each college and university. The likelihood of these policies changing anytime soon is slight, yet the convergence of on-campus sexual assault with gun rights is certainly getting more attention than ever. Do politicians truly care about curtailing sexual assault, or are they piggybacking gun rights onto an entirely different national issue?

Allowing the legal carry of firearms on college and university grounds is hardly a new idea. The national student-run organization Students for Concealed Carry began not long after the deadly 2007 Virginia Tech [Virginia Polytechnic Institute and State University] shooting as a way to lobby for not only Second Amendment rights, but also self-defense. The group advocates for legal concealed carry on all college campuses for students who are 21 years of age or older.

Pro-gun politicians have been framing the issue of arming female college students with a similar "good guy stopping a bad guy" philosophy: The only way to stop assailants is with a gun, so wouldn't it make sense to arm young women on college campuses? As Nevada state Rep. Michele Fiore, a pro-gun Republican, put it to the *Times*:

> If these young, hot little girls on campus have a firearm, I wonder how many men will want to assault them. The sexual assaults that are occurring would go down once these sexual predators get a bullet in their head.

To recap: A rapist, a woman with a gun, and a bullet to the head. What could possibly go wrong?

Self-defense measures have long been debated in feminist circles. While no one would say that it's wrong for a woman to defend herself against her rapist, some anti–sexual assault activists believe that placing so much attention on self-defense, whether its gun rights or women-centric martial arts classes, detracts from other forms of sexual assault prevention. Is the obvious answer here arming young women, or teaching people how to respect boundaries and the rights of others?

Sexual Assault, Guns, and Domestic Violence

What gun rights activists are leaving out of the conversation is the alarming link between intimate partner violence and gun deaths, indicating that some gun rights supporters might be looking at this issue with an outdated idea of when and how rape and sexual assault occur. According to statistics from the Department of Justice, approximately two-thirds of all rapes

The Problem with Guns as a Solution

Telling a potential rape victim to carry a gun isn't rape prevention. It's solution avoidance. These would-be remedies exacerbate the problem they purport to solve, making victims responsible for preventing their own attacks instead of putting the onus on rapists. Moreover, bills like this [a law permitting the legal carrying of loaded weapons on campus] deflect attention from most of the people who are committing rape: Depending upon which statistics you cite, anywhere from two-thirds to 80 percent of rapes are committed by someone the victim knows.

Jamil Smith,
"The Worst Way to Address Campus Rape,"
New Republic, *February 19, 2015.*

are committed by someone known to the victim, which is typically called "acquaintance rape," while four in 10 rapes occur in the victim's home. A large number of women, then, would be granting their rapist access to a gun, which in turn could be used against them.

It's not a stretch or hyperbole: Federal data have shown over the years that women have an increased risk of being the victim of intimate partner violence when a gun is in the home, or the perpetrator has access to a gun. In fact, women are three times more likely to be killed by an intimate partner when there is a gun in the home, according to research compiled by Johns Hopkins University.

A recent report from the Violence Policy Center, which tracks homicide and domestic violence, found that 93 percent of female homicide victims in 2012 were killed by an intimate partner; 52 percent of the female victims were killed with a gun, with the handgun being the most prevalent weapon involved.

"For individual women, we hope our study is a reminder to think very carefully about the facts before considering purchasing a gun for the purpose of self-protection," Violence Policy Center executive director Josh Sugarmann wrote in an article for the *Huffington Post* when the report was released. "The evidence shows that for women in America, just like men, guns are most often used not to save lives, but to take them."

While intimate partner violence is not always directly related to rape and sexual assault, data have shown that there's a clear overlap of physical and sexual violence. The most recent report on intimate partner violence from the Centers for Disease Control and Prevention shows that more than 14 percent of female victims have experienced rape, physical violence, and stalking.

And according to the Harvard Injury Control Research Center, women who reside in states with loose gun laws have elevated rates of unintentional gun deaths, firearm suicides, and firearm homicides than women who live in states with [fewer] guns.

A Solution, or Just Another Problem?

So, will arming young women actually prevent sexual violence and overall violence against women? Unfortunately, the success rates seem pitifully low. In one study published in the *American Journal of Public Health*, the researchers found after interviewing women at 67 domestic violence shelters in the United States, just 3 percent of women successfully used a handgun to defend themselves, while only 1 percent were able to injure their partners with a handgun. The women were much more likely to have the gun pointed in their direction.

Sexual assault and rape are violent crimes that might only turn more violent in the long run when guns are involved. Putting a "bullet in their [rapist's] head," as Fiore put it, is as much a fantasy, it seems, as rape being committed by an anonymous assailant on an unlit campus path.

> *"Callisto is the kind of tool you hope you'll never need—but for coeds everywhere, it couldn't be arriving at a better time."*

Prevention Apps May Be Key to Stopping Campus Sexual Assaults

Marissa Miller

In the following viewpoint, Marissa Miller argues that prevention applications on smartphones may be an effective way to address the campus sexual assault problem. Focusing on Callisto, a special app for reporting sexual assault, Miller asserts that apps can make it easier and less traumatic for survivors to report abuse and, by extension, help to prevent sexual assaults from happening in the first place. Miller is a journalist whose work has appeared in such publications as Cosmopolitan, *the* New York Times, VICE, *and* Reader's Digest Canada.

As you read, consider the following questions:

1. According to the viewpoint, how does Callisto work?

2. According to Callisto inventor Jessica Ladd, what was the impetus for the app's creation?

3. According to Miller, how does Callisto go beyond other methods of reporting sexual assault?

Sexual assaults on campus have never been a bigger topic than they are now, but coming forward to report your experience is still an incredibly draining experience. Luckily, change may be on the horizon by way of Callisto, an app set to launch at the beginning of the 2015 school year. It will allow students to report assaults through a digital portal in the comfort and safety of their own homes. "It seems there's a minority of people causing the vast majority of the problem, because reporting isn't happening," explains Callisto creator Jessica Ladd. "My main motivation is to make the whole process [of reporting] less traumatic. The prevention aspect is a happy consequence."

What Is Callisto?

Here's how Callisto works: You log on to the website, create a profile, provide photo evidence related to the assault (like text messages or photos), and fill out a questionnaire. You then have three options: a) the default, which securely saves your questionnaire in a time-stamped way and allows you to revisit it at any time; b) to report it to authorities directly; or c) to save it for now, and report your assault automatically once somebody else reports the same assailant. The purpose is to log information so that the system can view patterns across *all* reporting, and take a look at the larger trends. Additionally, sharing the experience privately is thought to be less traumatic for victims, making them more inclined to file a report in the first place.

"I know for myself that had Callisto been available when I was in college, I'd have chosen option C, mostly to back up their story and support their search for justice," says Ladd, who personally went through an assault. As she spoke to more and more survivors during the research phase of the app, she noticed all the aspects that mirrored her own experience. "I realized how many of the things that I went through that I thought were just me are actually common among us. That really reinforced the need for Callisto."

Callisto creates a safe space where victims can reach out to one another for support and help each other testify, but it also aims to help cement the event in history, in case your memory of the details falters. The recent *Rolling Stone* article about a girl named "Jackie," who claimed to have been gang-raped at UVA [University of Virginia], has come under severe criticism centering around whether or not the victim's allegations were accurate. As the story continues to unfold, one thing is crystal clear: Trauma can severely impair memory. And while Callisto may not be able to completely solve for recall issues, Ladd's hope is that by giving victims a platform to document the event ASAP, they can produce a stronger quality record of what happened, enhancing their credibility. The app also allows victims to work on their record over time as memories gradually resurface.

The goal isn't to wipe out third-party reporting completely, either. "I would love for in-person reporting to be survivor-friendly enough. I think that if sexual assault is happening regardless of your wonderful in-person resources, there's still a need for Callisto." In many ways, going online feels more natural. Plus, unlike the in-person option, Callisto provides the alternative of reporting only after someone else has pointed to the same perpetrator. While some schools and police forces have already implemented a policy of letting you know if there's another survivor whose experience mirrors your own, it's not yet a nationally streamlined system. Callisto fills that gap.

The Importance of Sexual Assault Apps

Of course, none of these [sexual assault apps] are perfect solutions.

They all depend on having a charged cell phone and enough signal to get a message out.

But they do provide students with a tangible tool that they previously lacked, and proponents say they can be part of a comprehensive approach by colleges to curb instances of rape and assault.

Juana Summers,
"Smartphone Apps Help to Battle Campus Sexual Assaults,"
NPR, August 13, 2014.

A Better Solution

Callisto is also a product with a lot of belief behind it: On Dec. 16 [2014], Google.org announced it will be funding the product. "We help entrepreneurs use technology to test out new solutions to big problems," says Jacquelline Fuller, director of Google.org. "Unfortunately, the epidemic of sexual assault on campus is one of those problems, and as the mother of two daughters currently in college, it hits particularly close to home. We are inspired by Jess Ladd and her team's commitment to empowering survivors of sexual assault by using information escrow to share critical information that could protect others in the future."

Sexual assault has unfortunately been a trending topic this year, from celeb allegations to on-campus assaults. Women are demanding better victim resources and pursuit practices, and more efficient reporting procedures ultimately help everyone involved. Callisto is the kind of tool you hope you'll never need—but for coeds everywhere, it couldn't be arriving at a better time.

"Do you need an anti-rape app at the ready? Is the solution to campus sexual violence on a smartphone? Experts in the field say the answers are complicated."

Prevention Apps Are Not an Effective Way to Stop Campus Sexual Assaults

Tara Culp-Ressler

In the following viewpoint, Tara Culp-Ressler argues that sexual assault prevention apps and other rape prevention technologies are not the best way to address the issue of sexual assault. Specifically, she contends that such methods are often produced by companies more interested in profits than results and that the technologies themselves generally fail to address the broader cultural concerns that are at the heart of the campus sexual assault problem. Culp-Ressler is health editor for ThinkProgress.

As you read, consider the following questions:

1. According to sexual assault activist Alexandra Brodsky, what is problematic about the way sexual assault prevention apps are distributed?

2. According to Culp-Ressler, how might the money being invested in the development of sexual assault prevention apps be better spent to combat sexual assault?

3. According to Culp-Ressler, how do the makers of sexual assault prevention apps misrepresent the realities of campus sexual assault?

Two weeks ago, a new nail polish that promised to detect date rape drugs took the media by storm. The product, developed by four male college students as a potential tool to address campus sexual assaults, sparked a passionate discussion about the most effective ways to tackle the issue. And although that conversation has since dissipated, the growing industry dedicated to anti-rape products has not.

"There's this entire little cottage industry of anti-rape solutions," Soraya Chemaly, a feminist writer and activist, told *ThinkProgress*. "It's clearly an identifiable market that's being pursued."

Inside Higher Ed recently used the exact same phrase—"cottage industry"—to refer to the growing number of safety apps being targeted at young people. At the end of August [2014], just in time for the beginning of the fall semester, the outlet reported that there are now dozens of smartphone tools for "worried college students" to download.

With so many new innovations, it may be difficult for the average American to wade through their options and figure out what's actually useful. Do you need an anti-rape app at the ready? Is the solution to campus sexual violence on a smartphone?

Experts in the field say the answers are complicated.

The Commodification of Sexual Assault

The first rule of thumb is to tread cautiously when it comes to what Chemaly calls the "commodification of sexual assault."

All of the rape prevention activists who spoke with *Think-Progress* expressed discomfort with the idea that the innovators in this field might be focused more on profiting than on ending rape. In their minds, resources to combat sexual assault shouldn't be for sale.

"I don't rule out the possibility that there could be an effective anti-rape effort that would take some sort of business model. That being said, it makes me really uncomfortable that there could be a tool that would only be accessible to some people depending on their ability to pay," Alexandra Brodsky, one of the founders and current codirectors of Know Your IX, a survivor-led group working to address campus sexual assault, said.

"It is sort of disturbing to me that there's this whole industry popping up, and there are definitely some products that seem like they're trying to exploit that," Nancy Schwartzman, who developed an app called Circle of 6 U to help colleges expand their sexual assault resources, added. "We've never been in it for the money."

There's also a question of where financial resources are best allocated. Student-led and grassroots efforts are already working on the ground to address campus violence. Online organizing campaigns are currently trying to focus attention on this issue. Victim advocate centers are struggling to get enough funding from colleges to keep on full-time staff members. Finding ways to effectively support the existing infrastructure may be more meaningful than pouring money into the next big smartphone app or roofie [slang for Rohypnol, a powerful sedative infamously nicknamed the "date rape drug"]-detecting coaster.

"Instead of raising $100,000 on a Kickstarter [crowdfunding platform] for the next anti-rape tool, let's put that money toward what it costs to process rape kits. Let's identify serial rapists," Chemaly said, pointing to the thousands of rape kits collecting dust because law enforcement departments don't have the resources to process them. "Let's start a Kickstarter for that!"

Addressing the Reality of Rape

One of the biggest issues with anti-rape innovations is that they often misrepresent the reality of sexual violence. A very tiny percentage of assaults, for example, involve the use of date rape drugs. Most college rapes occur between people who already know each other, at parties and in dorm rooms, not after a stranger jumps out of the bushes and accosts a girl on campus.

"The tricky thing is that this work is really counterintuitive in a lot of ways, and that means that well-meaning people can end up perpetuating myths about sexual violence in their attempt to stop the problem," Brodksy pointed out. "I think often these apps are designed for a narrative of violence that just isn't that prevalent. You have to ask, would this product have helped a student in the real world, as opposed to this sort of archetypal rape victim in a movie script?"

The people involved in efforts to develop new tools need to have done their homework, Brodsky says. They should either have conducted research into campus rape, consulted with survivors to get feedback about their proposal, or have personal experience themselves as a survivor of rape or an activist within the community.

Indeed, when developers take the time to learn more about how sexual assaults happen, their products end up looking a little different. For instance, Innovate Against Rape—a project housed in Carnegie Mellon University's Integrated Innovation Institution, which encourages people to come up with creative solutions to social problems—recently created two apps to give students more resources to report issues they see at parties. The apps, NightOwl and SPOT (A Problem), were developed after students did extensive research into campus sexual assaults.

"The people who you go to the party with are very important. So we've built our products around those bystanders," Donna Sturgess, the Integrated Innovation Institute's executive in residence, explained in an interview with *ThinkProgress*. "If you expect a woman, ahead of going to a party, to be doing things like putting pepper spray in her purse—all of those things actually don't work when they're in a social setting and out on the dance floor."

The key is creating resources for larger social settings, as well as including useful data like the contact information for the local rape crisis center, rather than "Big Brother" tools that promise to protect vulnerable women against the big bad strangers who might rape them.

"Does this app feel like it's the sort of patriarchal, paternalistic, police blue shield thing that says you need constant surveillance and protection? Or does the tool feel like something that's empowering, something you want to use, something that respects your privacy, something that's there to help you out?" Schwartzman said.

Can an App Challenge Rape Culture?

Anti-rape tools are often designed in a way that requires potential victims to be constantly vigilant—downloading apps, wearing special nail polish, and always thinking about ways to mitigate their risk of sexual assault. They're criticized for feeding into rape culture by assuming that it's women's responsibility to take extra steps to prevent rape.

Some advocates believe there's value in those technologies anyway. Scott Berkowitz, the president of the Rape, Abuse, and Incest National Network (RAINN), is one of those people. "I think the way that debate has gone has been unfortunate, because all crime prevention puts the onus on someone other than the perpetrator. It's vastly easier to affect the behavior of the good people than the bad," Berkowitz said. "Even bystander intervention programs, the kind of programs everyone is moving toward right now, put the onus on other people—I don't think that's a bad thing."

This past spring, RAINN made headlines for a similar criticism: Lamenting the "unfortunate trend towards blaming 'rape culture' for the extensive problem of sexual violence on campuses," which RAINN believes detracts from the emphasis on rapists' conscious choice to commit a crime.

Others firmly disagree. "Every solution is going to have its downsides, and that doesn't mean everything that's criticized should be totally cast off," Brodsky said. "But some of these tools, as we saw with the anti-rape nail polish, are only going to potentially help a tiny fraction of people—while also solidifying a really dangerous narrative of violence and of responsibility that is going to affect all people."

And some groups think they've found a way to carefully navigate that space. Schwartzman—whose Circle of 6 app allows users to select a group of six friends to easily contact if they wind up in a situation they need help getting out of—says her app can help facilitate culture change by requiring friends to discuss the responsibilities that come with being in each other's "circles." That requires them to broach the topic of healthy sexual relationships with peers and practice how to be an effective bystander in social situations.

"It's not just like, I need help and I'm going to get it because I have this mobile app," she explained. "You have six people who you've had a pretty in-depth conversation with about what it means to be accountable to each other—and those people might have six other people, and all of a sudden we're looking at these concentric circles of caring and community."

Chemaly thinks that's the key. "It's not as focused on personal responsibility—these types of tech innovations are actually engaged in challenging how we socialize," she said in reference to Circle of 6. "Nail polish doesn't do that at all."

Schwartzman and her colleagues also recently rolled out Circle of 6 U, a version of the app that can be tailored specifically for universities to offer students hyper-localized resources. They've already partnered with Williams College [in Massachusetts] and UCLA [University of California, Los Angeles], and are in talks with additional administrations that may be interested in bringing the app to their school. With that new focus, Schwartzman says the new app shifts the responsibility away from students protecting themselves and toward universities working to protect their students.

Shifting the Narrative

Many of the advocates who spoke to *ThinkProgress* agreed that, while technological innovations might be part of the larger fight against sexual violence, they're not a silver bullet to end rape.

"Sexual violence is a global systemic problem that is not going to be solved by pressing a button," Brodsky said. "If we shifted our outlook so that communities were actively calling out perpetrators and supporting survivors, we could see real social change. That is much larger than an app."

Others were more optimistic about technology's potential. "We want people to think about this as a fixable problem. Our interest is making the conversation bigger and louder," Donna Sturgess, who leads Innovate Against Rape, explained. "It's a clarion call to say, stand up for this issue and help us create solutions."

This industry typically serves as the nexus where very different worldviews about rape prevention end up clashing sharply. Often, the activists on the ground oppose what they see as ineffective tools that don't get to the heart of the deeper cultural problem. Meanwhile, the people who are excited about new innovations become frustrated that attempts to prevent sexual assault are being hampered by political correctness.

"It's really hard for some people to understand why anyone, and especially feminists, would reject a new product like anti-rape nail polish—how could you reject something that could help stop rape?" Chemaly said. "But those people are thinking about their individual safety, their children's safety, and not interested at all in attacking the systems that create the larger problem. That's not rape prevention, but rape avoidance."

As the recent coverage around the new nail polish demonstrates, broader society won't be coming to an agreement on the matter anytime soon. But there are perhaps less contentious ways to work on improving the way that society approaches sexual violence. Innovations don't necessarily have to focus on the prevention side. Efforts to ease the reporting process—something that survivors often say is traumatizing for them—could help encourage more people to file reports for incidences of sexual violence. For instance, a new reporting software program called Callisto, currently being developed with input from college rape survivors, seeks to give students more agency by allowing them to file an online report anonymously. It's been widely praised so far.

> *"By sharing the responsibility of hosting parties with sororities, it could take fraternities out of the hot seat when we talk about sexual assault."*

Sorority Parties Would Help Reduce Sexual Assaults on Campus

Sarah Robertson

In the following viewpoint, Sarah Robertson argues that allowing sororities to host parties might be an effective way to combat the campus sexual assault problem. She contends that when only fraternities are allowed to host parties, female students are forced into a dangerous situation where their risk of being sexually assaulted is particularly high. She adds that sorority parties would be a safer alternative and an easy way to address a very serious problem. At the time of writing, Robertson was a student at the University of Massachusetts Amherst.

As you read, consider the following questions:

1. According to Robertson, why do most sororities not currently host parties?

Sarah Robertson, "Coming to a Campus Near You: Sorority Parties," *The Radical Notion*, February 2, 2015. Copyright © 2015 Sarah Robertson. All rights reserved. Reproduced with permission.

2. According to Robertson, which sorority has already experimented with hosting its own parties, and how has that experiment worked?

3. According to Robertson, why is the concept of sorority-hosted parties merely a good idea and not a definitive solution to the campus sexual assault problem?

Imagine a fraternity party. A freshman girl arrives with some of her newfound friends. She gets too drunk and needs to lie down. Venturing upstairs out of the din and into the dark of an empty bedroom, a boy she was talking to earlier decides to help. He doesn't understand that she just wants to sleep. He doesn't see her stumble as she clings to the railing and spills beer on the sticky floor. The partygoers downstairs know nothing of what is going on behind closed doors. The two upstairs hardly have a clue either.

On January 19 [2015], Alan Schwarz of the *New York Times* published "Sorority Anti-Rape Idea: Drinking on Own Turf," to which Olga Khazan of the *Atlantic* responded [on January 21, 2015] with "The Pros and Cons of Sorority Parties." Both articles explored the idea of letting sororities host parties as a way to cut down on college sexual assault. The question on everyone's mind now is, "Why not give it a try?"

"I would definitely feel safer at a sorority party," said Dania Roach, a senior at George Washington University. "It's the home-court advantage."

The Status Quo

Currently the National Panhellenic Conference, an umbrella organization governing 26 sorority chapters nationwide, does not allow alcohol in sorority houses. The reason, according to Cindy H. Stellhorn, a broker at MJ Insurance, is because sorority houses pay lower insurance rates by not serving alcohol. For reasons unknown, fraternities have no problem covering the additional cost and hosting parties that are central to the nightlife of many campuses.

Sorority Parties and the Balance of Power

By having only fraternity men host parties, they are asserting dominance, making female guests submissive and reinforcing gender stereotypes.

If sororities could host parties and serve alcohol, this perpetuation of rape culture would be lessened because the playing field would be equal. Both men and women could host parties that serve alcohol, thus giving both fraternities and sororities equal social power.

Bekah Pollard,
"Why Can't Sorority Women Drink in Their Own Houses?,"
The Lala, March 26, 2015.

The double standard for sororities and fraternities is as deep-rooted in the fabric of Greek life as the institutions themselves. Those who argue to keep alcohol to the fraternities, a surprising 58 percent of respondents to a *Huffington Post* poll, say that they do not want to see things change.

"That's just the way it is," said a member of the Kappa Alpha fraternity in an interview with Schwarz. "We buy the alcohol, we serve the alcohol, they drink it. We all have a good time."

According to Kyle A. Pendleton, the director of harm reduction and education for Zeta Tau Alpha, sororities are more intimately decorated, therefore hosting parties would not be a good idea for them. Perhaps Mr. Pendleton would also argue that women are not smart enough or too faint of heart to host parties, too.

Men in Greek life are more likely to have committed rape and females who attend fraternity parties are more likely to have been sexually assaulted. Sororities often partner with fraternities for parties and events, always holding the gatherings in the fraternity houses. It is a match made in heaven for those content with the current status quo.

A Different Approach

Allowing sororities to host parties would be an experiment worth trying. In fact, one sorority with no national affiliation, Sigma Delta at Dartmouth College, has already done it. The sorority regularly hosts parties where they serve alcohol, and so far the experiment has gone quite well.

"Especially younger girls feel much more comfortable coming to our sisters for help if they need it, rather than men having almost all the power," said Molly Rickford, a social chair at the sorority. "That dynamic is one of the key reasons fraternity members feel so entitled to women's bodies, because women have no ownership of the social scene. You can't kick a guy out of his own house."

This could be great news for fraternities, too. By sharing the responsibility of hosting parties with sororities, it could take fraternities out of the hot seat when we talk about sexual assault.

This is not a solution, however, just a suggestion worth exploring. Sexual assault and sexism on campus will still manifest itself in students' lives as long as the current mentality surrounding women, partying, and drinking persists. Some could even argue that it is sexist to assume sororities will host more responsible parties simply because they are women. Binge drinking, for example, could grow as students party under a false sense of safety in sorority houses.

Remember the freshman girl from the party. Imagine, instead of the boy's bedroom, she stumbles into a sister's bedroom decked in posters and pink. Maybe there are already a few girls in there taking off their heels to nurse their tired feet. It has been a long night and it's too late for her to call a cab. She sleeps in the sister's room and leaves the next morning for a walk of shame more dignified than most.

Periodical and Internet Sources Bibliography

The following articles have been selected to supplement the diverse views presented in this chapter.

Erica Buist	"Can 'Sexual Consent' App Good2Go Really Reduce Assaults on Campus?," *Guardian*, September 30, 2014.
Maria Castellucci	"Keep Guns Out of the Campus Sexual Assault Battle," *Chicago Tribune*, February 26, 2015.
Andrea Flynn	"Guns on Campus: Not an Agenda for Women's Safety," *Next New Deal*, February 25, 2015.
Jaleesa Jones	"4 Free Apps to Help College Women Feel Safer," *USA Today*, June 1, 2014.
Tyler Kingkade	"The Answer to Campus Rape: More Guns, Say NRA-Backed Lawmakers," *Huffington Post*, March 12, 2015.
Kaitlin Mulhere	"Momentum for Campus Carry," *Inside Higher Ed*, March 30, 2015.
Alan Schwarz	"A Bid for Guns on Campuses to Deter Rape," *New York Times*, February 18, 2015.
Alan Schwarz	"Sorority Anti-Rape Idea: Drinking on Own Turf," *New York Times*, January 19, 2015.
Jamil Smith	"The Worst Way to Address Campus Rape," *New Republic*, January 19, 2015.
Juana Summers	"Smartphone Apps Help to Battle Campus Sexual Assaults," *NPR*, August 13, 2014.
Jonathan S. Tobin	"Concerned About Sexual Assaults on Campus? Let Women Defend Themselves," *Commentary*, February 19, 2015.

OPPOSING
VIEWPOINTS®
SERIES

What Other Factors Are Tied to the Campus Sexual Assault Problem?

Chapter Preface

Campus sexual assault is a broad, multifaceted topic that has social implications far beyond the basics of why it happens, how it is handled, and what can be done to change it. Of particular importance are the different social responses and reactions the problem elicits from various people across the sociopolitical spectrum. It is these responses and reactions that ultimately determine how the campus sexual assault problem is viewed and addressed on a cultural level.

The social concerns related to the campus sexual assault problem are many and varied. For example, there is much debate over whether the way media outlets report on campus sexual assault is helping to fight the problem or if it is only making it worse. Likewise, there is also heated debate over whether the federal government should be taking direct action in the fight against sexual assaults on campus or simply allowing colleges to deal with the matter on their own. There is even debate over the role of feminists in the campus sexual assault problem and whether their involvement is helpful or harmful.

In some cases, the social implications of the campus sexual assault problem arise from the actions taken to combat the issue. Perhaps the best example of this can be found in the idea of affirmative consent, or "yes means yes" laws. According to the definition established by the State University of New York, "affirmative consent is a clear, unambiguous, knowing, informed, and voluntary agreement between all participants to engage in sexual activity." In response to the campus sexual assault problem, numerous colleges—and even two states, namely California and New York, as of this writing—have adopted affirmative consent policies that require students who engage in intimate relations to verbally consent to sexual contact before proceeding with such activity. Each party is also required to ensure that consent is given throughout the entire act and must immediately stop if consent is revoked at any time. Further, most affirmative consent rules also specify that consent cannot be given if the consenting party is intoxicated, otherwise incapacitated, or under duress.

The implementation of affirmative consent has prompted a fierce social debate between supporters and critics. Supporters of the concept generally view affirmative consent as an effective way of addressing the campus sexual assault problem and an important step forward in recognizing the broader cultural issues at the heart of the problem. Critics, on the other hand, argue that affirmative consent is far more likely to make the problem worse by trivializing sexual violence and making sexual assault cases even harder for college officials to navigate than they already are. In the years to come, the way this debate plays out may well have a significant impact on the alleviation of the campus sexual assault problem.

The authors of the viewpoints in the following chapter examine several factors that are tied to the issue of sexual assault on campus, including affirmative consent, media representation of sexual assault incidents, and the role of feminist ideologies in combatting the problem.

> *"Which college community would you want for your daughter or son? One where sexual aggression or coercion is okay, as long as it does not entail physical force or the threats of force? Or one where your child is taught that sexual activity ought to be mutually agreed upon, unambiguously, by all parties?"*

Affirmative Consent Laws Are Necessary

Melanie Boyd and Joseph Fischel

In the following viewpoint, Melanie Boyd and Joseph Fischel argue in support of affirmative consent laws. The authors contend that colleges have an obligation to enforce broad disciplinary codes and assert that narrower codes—meaning those that only go so far as to match criminal statutes—leave students inadequately protected from the threat of sexual assault. Boyd is an assistant dean of student affairs and the director of the Office of Gender and Campus Culture at Yale University. Fischel, also part of the Yale faculty, is an assistant professor of women's, gender, and sexuality studies.

As you read, consider the following questions:

1. According to Boyd and Fischel, why is Jed Rubenfeld wrong when he says that his example "is not a law school hypothetical"?

2. According to the viewpoint, in what way does Jed Rubenfeld confuse college discipline and criminal justice?

3. According to Boyd and Fischel, why specifically must colleges have broad disciplinary policies?

How often have you had a family fight about university disciplinary codes at your holiday table? Rarely, we would guess, but this year [2014] might be an exception. Fueled by an alchemy of government regulation, student activism, and media coverage, we're in the midst of a heated national debate about university handling of sexual assault. Many of the fiercest arguments are about "affirmative consent": the choice of some schools to require the presence of ongoing agreement, not just the absence of refusal, in sexual encounters. Straightforward as it may seem, the affirmative consent standard has fueled widespread anxiety that otherwise promising young men will be branded as rapists for having had awkward sex.

The Rubenfeld Hypothesis

Take, for example, our colleague Jed Rubenfeld's recent sky-is-falling *New York Times* op-ed, "Mishandling Rape." Offering a mangled version of Yale's definition of sexual consent—the actual key terms are *positive, unambiguous, voluntary,* and *ongoing*—Rubenfeld sounds a panicked alarm:

> "Under this definition, a person who voluntarily gets undressed, gets into bed and has sex with someone, without clearly communicating either yes or no, can later say—correctly—that he or she was raped. This is not a law school hypothetical. The unambiguous consent standard requires this conclusion."

Rubenfeld errs twice. First: This can *only* be a law school hypothetical. Real people, having sex in real life, communicate constantly. And what's more, that communication works. Determining consent *post facto* in a disciplinary hearing may be difficult (and disciplinary boards will sometimes get it wrong), but *in media res* [in the middle of the act] agreement is clear. Sexual cues may be nuanced, but they are manifold and familiar. People lean in or pull away. They intensify or slow down. They use verbal and nonverbal signals familiar from everyday life to collaborate in mutual initiation—or to evade, ignore, and reject propositions. In sexual and nonsexual contexts, people are highly skilled at discerning between rejection and acceptance, and they know when signals are too ambiguous to make a solid call. "Affirmative consent" is neither a feminazi trap nor a presumption of guilt. It is an accurate description of what we do when we are having sex that is not abusive or coerced: We seek confirmation that our partner is a willing participant.

Rubenfeld's second error: He provocatively confuses college discipline and criminal justice, repeatedly referencing "rape trials" when what he really means are "sexual misconduct disciplinary board hearings." The central question in a "rape trial" is: Did the defendant commit a crime? The central question before a university sexual misconduct hearing is: Did the respondent violate the school's sexual misconduct policy? Sexual misconduct is a *far* more expansive category than "rape," incorporating criminal acts alongside noncriminal behaviors that are nonetheless at odds with community standards—standards like nondiscrimination and sex equality. The penalties are also vastly different. To be judged guilty in a criminal court can lead to imprisonment. To be found responsible in a disciplinary hearing will lead, at most, to expulsion from the community.

Colleges and universities must respond to crimes, of course, but their obligations extend well beyond. Why must

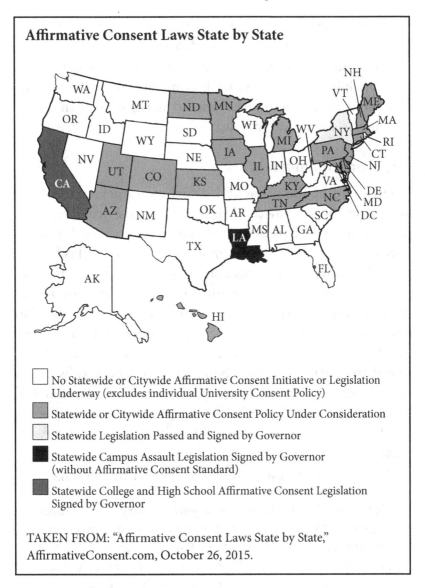

Affirmative Consent Laws State by State

☐ No Statewide or Citywide Affirmative Consent Initiative or Legislation Underway (excludes individual University Consent Policy)

▨ Statewide or Citywide Affirmative Consent Policy Under Consideration

☐ Statewide Legislation Passed and Signed by Governor

■ Statewide Campus Assault Legislation Signed by Governor (without Affirmative Consent Standard)

▨ Statewide College and High School Affirmative Consent Legislation Signed by Governor

TAKEN FROM: "Affirmative Consent Laws State by State," AffirmativeConsent.com, October 26, 2015.

disciplinary codes be so broad? Our education mission demands it, as do various federal and state laws and regulations. Students, faculty, and staff are entitled to a campus free of harassment, discrimination, or other obstacles to their full participation in the learning community. Sexual misconduct—including noncriminal misconduct—creates many of the most common impediments to full educational access, and thus must be addressed by campus authorities.

Rubenfeld disagrees, arguing that schools should shrink their disciplinary codes to match criminal statutes. "Sexual assault on campus," he writes, "should mean what it means in the outside world and in courts of law."

The Consequences

What would be the social and sexual consequences if we followed Rubenfeld's advice, if universities jettisoned affirmative consent and abandoned their efforts to quash sexual misconduct as practices of sex discrimination and inequality? Many states, including Connecticut, still require "force" or "threat of force" as an element of the crime of rape or sexual assault. Indeed, in a law journal article published last year, Rubenfeld advocates just such a definition, proposing that consent be mostly excised from criminal law. (He makes an exception for agreed-to violent or BDSM [bondage, dominance, sadism, and masochism] sex.) What rape violates is not sexual autonomy, he argues, but a right to bodily self-possession, a right abrogated only by force—overpowering, pinning down, imprisonment, etc.—or threats of force.

Let us offer our own hypothetical to clarify the stakes:

Cary and Nat are dancing at a party, having a few drinks. They kiss. They walk back to Cary's room, get undressed, and get into bed. They're both into it. But then, Nat (a) rolls over and falls asleep, (b) says "I'd rather just make out tonight and save sex for a more sober time" and pulls away, or (c) says "no, please stop" and curls up in a ball. Cary takes no notice and proceeds to have penetrative sex with Nat.

In Rubenfeld's Yale law journal world, none of these scenarios should count as rape or sexual assault. In Rubenfeld's *NYT* op-ed world, none of these scenarios should even count as campus sexual misconduct. Perhaps reasonable people will disagree about the appropriate descriptions for these acts, and whether and to what degree each should qualify as a crime. But we think it is entirely reasonable for a university to state, unequivocally, that these sexual encounters are anathema to a community principled on free and equal participation. Why should sex premised on mutuality, respect, and joint agreement—rather than sex premised on pressure, intimidation, and acquiescence—be an administratively endorsed, and administratively enforced, standard?

After all, which college community would you want for your daughter or son? One where sexual aggression or coercion is okay, as long as it does not entail physical force or the threats of force? Or one where your child is taught that sexual activity ought to be mutually agreed upon, unambiguously, by all parties?

> "[Under affirmative consent laws,] the burden of proof will fall on the accused, usually a male student. It becomes his responsibility to demonstrate that he received consent, a nearly impossible feat, and without the right to the presumption of innocence afforded in criminal courts."

Affirmative Consent Laws Are a Bad Idea

Masha Gershman

In the following viewpoint, Masha Gershman argues that affirmative consent laws are an unfair way to address the college sexual assault problem. She contends that such laws, intended to reduce the incidence of sexual assault by requiring both parties to clearly establish consent prior to engaging in sexual activity and ensure that consent is given throughout the act, unfairly target accused individuals and make it unnecessarily difficult for them to defend themselves against assault accusations. Gershman is a Massachusetts-based writer.

As you read, consider the following questions:

1. According to Gershman, why are the California affirmative consent law's guidelines relating to consent and intoxication problematic?

2. According to Gershman, why is it unfair for campus tribunals to adjudicate sexual assault cases?

3. According to Gershman, why is it more dangerous for campus tribunals, rather than criminal courts, to adjudicate sexual assault cases?

Two college students lie on a dorm room bed, there are soft whispers and light touching, but escalating passions are abruptly interrupted when one student hands the other a sexual consent form. The students' lawyers, suddenly revealed to be sitting on either side of the bed, dive into heated negotiations over what sexual activities will and will not transpire that evening. That comical video was produced in 2004, but it may seem less absurd now than it did a decade ago.

The Reality of Affirmative Consent

California's "affirmative consent" bill, signed into law by Gov. Jerry Brown last month [September 2014], sets a new, strict framework for how college students can engage in sexual activity. According to the bill, it is the responsibility of all parties involved to seek either verbal or nonverbal consent. According to Jessica Pride, a sexual assault lawyer, verbal consent can be a simple yes, or an "uhuh." Nonverbal can include nodding one's head or removing one's clothes. That's a fairly standard understanding of consent. But the bill also requires that consent be ongoing, and specifies that it can be revoked at any time, marking a departure from traditional practice. Barring incapacitation or force, courts typically follow a "no means no" standard, meaning that if one person tries a sexual move that his partner doesn't appreciate, it is the partner's obligation to make that known. And then his immediate responsibility to stop.

"Affirmative consent requires that you get consent before you do something. . . . So if one [partner] touches another, and the other person says 'I'm not in the mood,' they've already committed sexual assault," says Joe Cohn, legislative and policy director for the Foundation for Individual Rights in Education (FIRE). "If you don't ask before you do the next thing, you've already violated the rule." In other words, when two college students engage in sexual activity, any change within that activity—a change of position or rhythm for example, behavior that tends to progress naturally—must now first be granted permission. Otherwise, whoever initiated the change could technically face assault claims.

The bill also states that intoxication automatically prevents people from being able to grant consent, regardless if they do so verbally or otherwise. But the definition of intoxication is vague, and the way schools and individuals perceive it varies. Generally, it hinges on incapacitation, namely, whether or not an individual can appreciate what's happening to him or her. According to Cohn, incapacitation can include if someone is "totally wasted, drugged against their will, hit on the head with a brick" or is underage. Pride defines the threshold as whether an individual can get behind the wheel of a car and drive. Elena Koukina, a graduate student at the University of California, Berkeley, says that at a recent workshop, the line of intoxication was described as, "if that question even arises in your mind then they're too drunk."

Let's not forget, however, that this law applies to colleges, where the reality is that a lot of students get drunk, and a lot of students have sex when they do. According to Pride, alcohol has been a factor in most of her cases. So if intoxication precludes the possibility of consent, and if the threshold of intoxication varies, then many students can potentially find themselves in dangerous territory. Supporters of the bill, like Sarah Green, Title IX officer at Gonzaga University, believe that it eliminates ambiguity and serves to educate students about appropriate sexual interactions. "It opens the dialogue more and it gives a real framework for what appropriate sexual relationships should be. And you don't get the ambiguous, 'well, she didn't say no so it was consent,'" Green says. Dianne Klein, assistant media relations director at the University of California [UC] Office of the President, says that the UC system adopted the affirmative consent standard before the bill was passed in order to "educate students and faculty and staff on their responsibilities. And [to] encourage survivors to report [what happened to them] because it provides clear definitions, and allows them to judge whether what happened to them was sexual assault."

But it seems that the bill has the potential to generate much more confusion, and create many more problems than the ones it eliminates. Cynthia Garrett is an attorney who lobbied against the bill. According to her, the "revoked at any time" clause can be especially problematic: "This bill doesn't require any protest, or a victim to say no. The consent has to be ongoing and can be revoked at any time. What if she revokes it in the middle of the act and doesn't have to say anything—how is he supposed to know?" Most cases will be, like those of decades past, matters of "he said, she said." What is new, however, is that the burden of proof will fall on the accused, usually a male student. It becomes his responsibility to demonstrate that he received consent, a nearly impossible feat, and without the right to the presumption of innocence afforded in criminal courts.

The Legal Consequences of Affirmative Consent

Here's where the feds come in. When a claim is raised on college campuses, it will be handled by the procedure outlined in a 2011 edict issued by the Department of Education's Office for Civil Rights (OCR). It not only obligates universities to independently handle cases of sexual misconduct, but also prescribes how these investigations and deliberations must be run. Campus tribunals are expected to use the "preponderance of evidence" standard, the lowest possible burden of proof, normally reserved for civil matters involving money or property. In other words, a student would have to be shown "more likely than not" to have committed the crime in order to be found guilty.

The edict also all but eradicates due process. Hearsay counts as evidence. Cross-examination of the accuser is barred, for fear of traumatizing him or her further. While in some schools a lawyer or advocate for each student is permitted to be present, he or she is usually not allowed to speak. "Even in civil law you have protections for lower standards of proof, physical evidence, cross-examination. Cross-examination isn't to intimidate somebody, it's to allow a jury or a judge to assess their demeanor. That's a factor in determining truth," says Garrett. "There are expert witnesses, criminal psychologists who are experienced in this. [Lawyers] question each juror to make sure they'll be unbiased before they sit on the jury," she continues. "There is all kinds of overlay to ensure that a person is presumed innocent until proven guilty."

On college campuses, cases are investigated by campus police, Title IX officers, and faculty members. But it's unclear whether they are properly trained to perform such investigations. Green says that Title IX representatives at her university receive training from various presenters on the law's requirements. According to Klein, the UC system offers extensive training, including "what constitutes as a violation of policy, and how [to] deal with somebody who's been traumatized." But those involved in the investigation aren't judges, lawyers, criminal investigators, or specialists in sexual assault. "You're taking these very complex cases, handing them over to someone who got trained for a week and who doesn't need to use evidence," Garrett says.

Then there is the question of objectivity. Faculty, Title IX officers, and other representatives of the university also deliberate and issue verdicts. And they are undoubtedly aware of the fact that their employer can lose its federal funding if it is found to have violated Title IX by mishandling a case. They have skin in the game, which jurors never do.

FIRE's Joe Cohn raises a different issue. While campus proceedings aren't criminal cases, they do have criminal law implications. According to Cohn, anything a student says during an investigation is admissible against him in a criminal court, which is true for any public statements individuals make. The only exception is when an individual was compelled to make those statements. "Technically speaking, student statements in campus judiciaries aren't compelled because students can always choose to withdraw from the school and not face the tribunal," Cohn says. But if they do choose to speak in the tribunal, they face a situation where they are responsible for proving their innocence without the representation of a lawyer and without the protection of due process. "So, practically speaking, students are being forced to waive their 5th Amendment rights in order to defend themselves on campus."

If false accusations are negligible or nonexistent, then these gaps in the bill are nothing to worry about. And, as Pride explains in reference to the shift in burden of proof, even if a student is found responsible, the punishment doesn't mean jail time. "Does it mean that more people will be found guilty? Potentially, but in the worst case they get kicked out of school." But false accusations do happen, and whatever their number they are not so easily brushed aside. If someone is falsely accused and subsequently expelled, what happens next?

The Problem with Affirmative Consent

The campus crusade against rape has achieved a major victory in California with the passage of a so-called "yes means yes" law. Unanimously approved by the state Senate yesterday [in August 2014] after a 52–16 vote in the assembly on Monday, SB967 requires colleges and universities to evaluate disciplinary charges of sexual assault under an "affirmative consent" standard as a condition of qualifying for state funds. The bill's supporters praise it as an important step in preventing sexual violence on campus. In fact, it is very unlikely to deter predators or protect victims. . . .

Many . . . say that affirmative consent is not about getting permission but about making sure sexual encounters are based on mutual desire and enthusiasm. No one could oppose such a goal. But having the government dictate how people should behave in sexual encounters is hardly the way to go about it.

Cathy Young,
"Campus Rape: The Problem with 'Yes Means Yes,'"
Time, *August 29, 2014.*

The Practical Consequences of Affirmative Consent

Sherry Warner-Seefeld and Judith Grossman can answer that question. Both women's sons were falsely accused of sexual misconduct, and both have firsthand experience of the campus tribunal process. Sherry's son Caleb was a student at the University of North Dakota [UND] when charges of sexual assault were brought against him by another student, a woman with whom he'd had a relationship a few months prior. Eleven days later, Caleb sat before a university tribunal, facing the dean and a number of other high-level university administrators. Within a few hours, Caleb was found guilty and immediately expelled. His transcript indicated expulsion due to sexual assault, significantly diminishing his chances of transferring to another university.

Soon after, the local police department opened its own investigation into Caleb's case and found, three months later, that Caleb's accuser had falsified her report. A warrant was filed for his accuser's arrest. She fled to California, and the case remains open. Shortly after the police department's finding, Warner-Seefeld approached the university to clear her son of the charges against him. The university refused for nearly a year, citing various bureaucratic stipulations. Not until Warner-Seefeld attracted significant publicity did UND comply. Caleb had waited nearly 18 months for his name and transcript to be cleared of a false charge. He never went back to school.

Grossman's son, whose identity she won't reveal, was accused of sexual misconduct by an ex-girlfriend, and the alleged incident had occurred three years earlier. Her son received a list of allegations that were so vague as to "render any defense virtually impossible," she says. Eventually, though he was not granted a finding of innocence, he was not convicted, good fortune which Grossman says is due more to her own determination and resources than the competence of those sitting on the tribunal.

This summer, Warner-Seefeld and Grossman launched Families Advocating for Campus Equality (where Garrett sits on the board of directors) to raise awareness about developments on college campuses and to provide support for families in situations similar to their own. Warner-Seefeld says she has already received 35 calls from families whose sons were accused—they say falsely—since August. Garrett keeps records of lawsuits brought by students who claim they were falsely accused. She has identified 49 such cases since 2011, and her list is growing.

But the numbers aren't important. The question is whether the practices that universities have in place are fair, and whether they actually serve to make campuses safer for students. At worst, if an innocent person is found responsible, he or she will be expelled. Pride is right about that. But gaining acceptance to another university, not to mention having access to the kinds of jobs available to those with a college degree, becomes that much more difficult, if not impossible.

The situation is especially dire if a guilty person is (rightly) expelled, Cohn emphasizes. In this case, the perpetrator doesn't go behind bars but is released back into the world, free to repeat the assault. And the new focus and push toward campus tribunals makes criminal convictions much more difficult. "Prosecutors and police chiefs across the country have told me they have only 72 hours to get a rape kit done. . . . After that period of time, all of that physical evidence is gone. [If universities tell students,] 'the criminal justice system won't help you, here's another avenue,' a number of meritorious claims will be diverted to campus. That is a recipe for guaranteeing that violent predators are on the street."

But the system of handling claims seems to be permanently embedded in the collegiate framework, and the affirmative consent bill is gaining momentum. Versions are being adopted or proposed in New York, New Hampshire, and New Jersey. Male students might be wise to, quite literally, hang on to their britches.

> *"The White House ... task force report on campus sexual assaults ... reflects a presumption of guilt in sexual assault cases that practically obliterates the due process rights of the accused."*

Federal Government Intervention in the Campus Sexual Assault Crisis Is Flawed

Wendy Kaminer

In the following viewpoint, Wendy Kaminer argues that the federal government's approach to the campus sexual assault problem has been deeply flawed and severely unbalanced. She contends that the Barack Obama administration's policies heavily favor alleged victims and unfairly target the accused. She holds that any legal guidelines for handling campus sexual assault cases that do not protect the rights of both parties cannot truly be effective. Kaminer is a lawyer, author, and social critic.

As you read, consider the following questions:

1. According to Kaminer, why is it wrong to bar cross-examination in campus sexual assault proceedings?

2. What standard of proof are colleges required to meet to judge the accused individual guilty in campus sexual assault cases, according to the viewpoint?

3. According to Kaminer, in what way do media outlets fail when it comes to reporting on "believe the victim" biases?

"Not Alone," the White House entitled its task force report on campus sexual assaults. "Believe the Victim," the report might as well have been called. It reflects a presumption of guilt in sexual assault cases that practically obliterates the due process rights of the accused. Students leveling accusations of assault are automatically described as "survivors" or "victims" (not alleged victims or complaining witnesses), implying that their accusations are true.

When you categorically presume the good faith, infallible memories and entirely objective perspectives of self-identified victims, you dispense with the need for cumbersome judicial or quasi-judicial proceedings and an adversary model of justice. Thus the task force effectively prohibits cross-examination of complaining witnesses: "The parties should not be allowed to cross-examine each other," the report advises, denying the fundamental right to confront your accuser.

Alleged victims are supposed to be protected from "hurtful questioning." The impulse to protect actual victims from the ordeal of a cross-examination by their attackers is laudable. But by barring cross-examination, you also protect students who are mistaken or lying, and you victimize (even traumatize) students being falsely accused.

School officials are also encouraged to substitute a "single investigator" model for a hearing process, which seems a prescription for injustice. As the Foundation for Individual Rights in Education [FIRE] points out, pursuant to this model, "a sole administrator would be empowered to serve as detective, judge and jury, affording the accused no chance to challenge his or her accuser's testimony."

Addressing Sexual Assault on Campus

These "reforms" exacerbate an already dangerously unreliable approach to evaluating charges of assault. In 2011, the Department of Education issued guidelines requiring colleges and universities to employ a minimal "preponderance of evidence" standard in cases involving allegations of harassment or violence. This is the lowest possible standard of proof, which merely requires discerning a 50.01 percent chance that a charge is more likely than not to be true. It facilitates findings of guilt, which will be merited in some cases, and not others. For students wrongly accused, the consequences of a guilty finding can be as dire as a not guilty finding for students actually victimized.

These are difficult, potentially traumatizing cases for all parties involved, and not surprisingly some students complaining of sexual assault prefer not to participate in investigations or hearings. How do you evaluate their claims? If you're the White House task force, you simply presume that they're true: "Where a survivor does not seek a full investigation, but just wants help to move on, the school needs to respond there too." Move on from having "survived" precisely what? You can sympathize with a victimized student who doesn't want to pursue a claim and still wonder how school officials can respond fairly and intelligently to an accusation that hasn't been investigated and may or may not be true.

Does this approach exaggerate or trivialize the problem at hand? Sexual assault is a serious felony, the task force and victim advocates would agree. According to the administration, one in five students is victimized by it. Assume that estimate is accurate and imagine that 20 percent of the people in a community are suffering violent assaults. Residents would likely demand a stronger police presence and stepped-up criminal prosecutions, rather than informal neighborhood councils to "adjudicate" complaints. But on campus, felony complaints are to be prosecuted informally, the way schools might prosecute violations of a dress code, without affording accused students any meaningful rights.

Justifications for this include the particular ambiguities of sexual assault charges on campus. Alleged assaults often involve alcohol, actual victims may know their attackers and, in a closed campus community, may be hesitant to press accusations against them. The irony is that these factors complicating the prosecution of campus assaults and inspiring calls for informal, non-adversarial responses to them are the same factors that, as victim advocates rightly assert, have encouraged victim blaming and prevented law enforcement authorities from taking allegations of campus assaults seriously.

A Better Solution

The solution to the problem of ignoring sexual assault charges shouldn't be assuming that they're true. The "believe the victim" biases underlying the White House task force report aren't subtle or inconsequential, but they're not generally recognized by left-of-center media. The occasional students' rights watchdog, like Brooklyn College professor KC Johnson, offers a critical, in-depth analysis of the administration's approach, but in general reactions are dictated by partisan or ideological biases: The right has its own politically correct mandate to oppose any Obama administration civil rights initiative. The left labors under a pop feminist mandate to reflexively believe self-identified victims of sexual assault.

Similar assumptions about victimization often dictate how people view the rights of the accused and their accusers. Compare the administration's disregard for due process in formulating disciplinary procedures for campus sexual misconduct complaints to its critique of harsh, due process–less disciplinary practices in elementary and secondary schools.

School discipline tends to be discriminatory, at least in effect, targeting racial and ethnic minorities, so civil rights advocates outside the administration are rallying against it, rightly seeking due process protections for students accused. But in response to allegations of sexual misconduct in colleges and universities, the same advocates generally favor a prosecutorial approach that sacrifices due process over protections for presumed victims.

How do we account for these opposing approaches to student rights? Considering elementary and secondary school disciplinary practices, the administration sympathizes with students accused. In campus sexual assault cases, it sympathizes with accusers. But rights shouldn't be allocated on the basis of subjective sympathies, unless we want to encourage discrimination—the sort of discrimination that plagues minority students in public schools. Every student accused of a crime or disciplinary infraction has an equal right to due process and fair adjudication of charges. You're also "Not Alone," the administration should guarantee students accused of sexual assault. You're accompanied by fundamental rights.

> "The time is right and ripe to confront and perhaps change the fusty way journalists handle sexual assault."

Media Coverage of Campus Sexual Assaults Should Be More Aggressive

Jamie Stiehm

In the following viewpoint, Jamie Stiehm argues that we need to have better, more frequent media coverage of college sexual assaults. She contends that, at present, journalists are underreporting on the subject and thereby allowing the problem to quietly continue. She says that more media coverage would bring more attention to the campus sexual assault problem and make it more difficult for rapists to victimize others. Stiehm is a weekly Creators Syndicate columnist. Her op-eds on politics, culture, and history have appeared in newspapers across the nation, including in the New York Times *and the* Washington Post. *She previously worked as a reporter at the* Baltimore Sun *and* The Hill. *Stiehm's first journalism job was as an assignment editor at the CBS News bureau in London.*

As you read, consider the following questions:

1. According to Stiehm, what was the upside of the much criticized *Rolling Stone* story on the alleged rape of "Jackie" at the University of Virginia?

2. Why did Geneva Overholser believe that sexual assault cases should be reported on more aggressively?

3. According to Stiehm, why are so many college sexual aggressors able to get away with assaulting other students?

So sorry, *Rolling Stone* has brought journalism to a hard pass: how to cover stories of rape, especially those that happen on college campuses? The magazine's sensational account of a gang-rape scene at a fraternity house crumbled under close scrutiny. The story relied on the alleged victim identified only as "Jackie." The writer did not contact any of the young men that she accused as her attackers. The case never went to court. The editors apologized (twice) for poor journalistic judgment after they concluded (too late) that Jackie's account was not credible.

But look at it this way. Even with its flaws, her story struck a chord. As Julia Horowitz, the assistant managing editor of the *Cavalier Daily*, wrote in *Politico* magazine: "Yes, the story was sensational. But even the most sensational story, it seems, can contain frightening elements of truth." As badly as the editors botched this story, the sense of urgency over sexual assault was and is real. The time is right and ripe to confront and perhaps change the fusty way journalists handle sexual assault. There is a mounting sense of crisis among young people, a churn and a debate that we in the news profession need to keep up with. Sexual assault is also high in the military, which recorded roughly 19,000 reports this year [2014], a decrease from a whopping 26,000 in 2012. Many of these cases involve

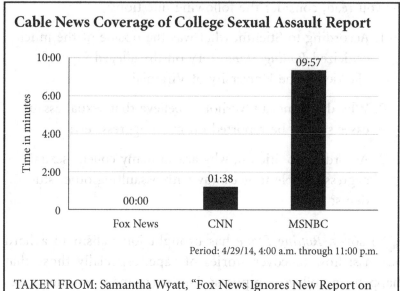

Cable News Coverage of College Sexual Assault Report

Period: 4/29/14, 4:00 a.m. through 11:00 p.m.

TAKEN FROM: Samantha Wyatt, "Fox News Ignores New Report on College Sexual Assault," Media Matters for America, April 30, 2014.

young women as well who may feel reluctant, deployed in a fort far from home or out on a ship, to report an abuser, especially if he's in her chain of command.

Let me suggest the following. Listen up, editors: At some point, rape reporting has to be done in daylight, with names, faces and voices. Geneva Overholser, a high priestess of newspaper journalism who recently stepped down as the director of the USC [University of Southern California] Annenberg School [for Communication and] Journalism, has said so for years. As she put it in a *New York Times* op-ed way back in 1989, "Does not our very delicacy in dealing with rape victims subscribe to the idea that rape is a crime of sex rather than the crime of brutal violence that it really is? Surely the sour blight of prejudice is best treated by being subjected to strong sunlight." For more justice and credibility, rape victims must tell their stories in a public forum. There is nothing to be ashamed of: Put it on the public record and break the silences that keep shame alive.

Further, the government is acting more decisively than it ever has. This spring, rape became a red-hot issue at 85 universities and colleges across the country as they came under a major federal investigation for how they handle cases of sexual violence. There are a lot of elite private and public institutions on that list, including Swarthmore College (my alma mater), Amherst College and the University of Chicago.

For now, college-age women remain as vulnerable in an atmosphere more highly charged with rape in the cultural conversation as ever before.

These attacks happen in a netherworld, a landscape beyond the reach of courts and newspapers. If the victim is a first-year student, she may not know where to turn for medical help or law enforcement. Her shame, secrecy and silence empower the perpetrators. They rely on a code of silence. The perpetrators depend on victims being stunned or shamed into silence, into not telling authorities, so they can carry on with impunity—a darker twist on sex and drugs and rock and roll. I believe the need to change the code extends to journalism, which fails to cover rape like any other violent crime. We should demystify the way we deal with rape, period.

If we dared to try the new method first proposed by Overholser, then society could see how commonplace rape is—hurting our own sisters, daughters, mothers, wives. It simply must come out into the open eventually and not be stigmatized as if by a medieval shroud. We can also get a clearer picture of the doers. *Rolling Stone* could have done a real public service by getting the truth straight on the record. Instead, the story is a cautionary one in how feeble and futile our notions are when it comes to reporting rape.

Remember, social silences empower victimizers, whether in public or private.

> "The media love crisis, and hyping sexual assault is a good way to get attention."

Media Coverage of Campus Sexual Assaults Only Worsens the Problem

John Stossel

In the following viewpoint, John Stossel argues that media outlets are exaggerating the campus sexual assault problem and are only making it worse in the process. He contends that the media's eagerness to use campus sexual assault to attract attention is causing a distortion of the facts and leading people to believe the problem is worse than it really is. This, Stossel says, trivializes campus sexual assault and makes the situation worse for everyone. Stossel is an award-winning print and television journalist who hosts a weekly news show on the Fox Business channel.

As you read, consider the following questions:

1. According to Stossel, how did *Rolling Stone* violate the principles of journalistic integrity in reporting on the alleged University of Virginia rape case?

2. According to Stossel, how has President Obama made the campus sexual assault problem worse?

3. What does Stossel say are the potential consequences of blurring the lines of violent and nonviolent contact in relation to sexual assault?

Apparently, new laws are needed because at colleges, sexual assault is "epidemic." Rape is so common that there is a "rape culture."

I hear that a lot.

It is utter exaggeration. Fortunately, AEI [American Enterprise Institute for Public Policy Research] scholar Christina Hoff Sommers is around to reveal the truth.

The Reality of "Rape Culture"

"This idea of a rape culture was built on false statistics and twisted theories about toxic masculinity," she says.

No one denies that some men, especially when drunk, get violent and abusive. I saw nasty behavior when I was in college, and I assume there are places worse than Princeton.

Sommers says, "I always make clear, rape is a very serious problem, (but) if you look at the best data . . . it is not an epidemic. And we do not have a rape culture."

The difference is not just numbers, she says. "Rape culture means everything in society is reinforcing (rape) and making it seem a legitimate thing to do. Of course that's not true."

The media love crisis, and hyping sexual assault is a good way to get attention.

Rolling Stone and UVA

Recently, a *Rolling Stone* article said that men routinely assault women at the University of Virginia [UVA]. It told a frightening story, based on one witness, of gang rape in a frat house that left the victim's friends completely uninterested, since assault is so routine.

The article got lots of attention. Then completely fell apart.

The Exaggeration of College Rape Culture

Elizabeth Bartholet, an expert on civil rights and family law as well as a feminist, made a powerful "have-you-no-shame Senator" observation: "I believe that history will demonstrate the federal government's position to be wrong, that our society will look back on this time as a moment of madness."

Rape crisis activists believe this madness serves a worthy purpose: It dramatizes a real problem. Whatever the numbers, far too many women are being harmed. As Ezra Klein says, "Ugly problems don't always have pretty solutions." But this is exactly wrong. We know from objective research, and some of us know from experience, that sexual assault, although not epidemic, *is* a serious problem on campus, and victims too often suffer in silence.

But hysteria over a rape culture sheds no light and produces no solutions. Panic breeds chaos and mob justice. It claims innocent victims, undermines social trust, and distracts attention from genuine cases of abuse.

Christina Hoff Sommers,
"The Media Is Making College Rape Culture Worse,"
Daily Beast, January 23, 2015.

"It proved to be a sort of gothic fantasy, a male-demonizing fantasy," says Sommers. "It was absurd."

In much American media, a rape story is "too good to check." The *Rolling Stone* author admits she wanted to believe. She barely fact-checked the claims made by her source. Her source's story fit the reporter's own "rape culture" narrative. She interviewed students at many campuses, waiting for the rape story she wanted to hear.

The *Rolling Stone* story sounded extraordinary from the beginning.

"But for several days, people in the media just believed it, and publicized it, and anguished over it," says Sommers. To doubt was taboo. "The hysteria around campus assault, the false information has been building for so long," warns Sommers, "people are willing to believe anything."

Overreaction and Misinformation

President [Barack] Obama added to the misinformation by pandering to the feminist victim lobby, creating a "sex abuse task force" and repeating a widely quoted—yet obviously absurd—rape statistic. "It is estimated that one in five women on college campuses has been sexually assaulted during their time there. One in five!"

Yes, Mr. President, we hear that a lot.

But it's a lie.

At allegedly horrible University of Virginia, where *Rolling Stone* said assault was routine, 46 sexual offenses were reported per thousand students. That's 46 too many, but for "one in five" to be true, it would have to be 200.

Admittedly, many victims of assault fear going public, so the UVA number may be higher than 46. Nevertheless, one in five just isn't plausible.

"The figure is closer to one in 50," says Sommers of colleges overall.

The Way We Approach Sexual Assault

Sexual assault is serious stuff. Activists trivialize it by asking survey questions like, "Did you ever receive unwanted sexual contact while drunk?" and counting "yes" answers as assaults.

"The CDC [Centers for Disease Control and Prevention] did a study," recounts Sommers. "They called it sexual violence if you said yes (to the question) 'Has anyone ever pressured you to have sex by telling you tales, or making you feel guilty?' *That* counted as violence."

It's not nice to pressure someone. But people do that. That's different from violence, isn't it?

If we forget the difference between violent and nonviolent conduct, no one is safe. If we pretend everyone is guilty instead of a few real criminals, rapists win. No longer are they a dangerous group of very bad people, they're just—men.

That's no victory for women. Or anyone.

"On every single college campus in the United States, there is a powerful, committed group of feminists and feminist allies who are working to prevent sexual violence and respond to the needs of survivors."

Feminists and Feminist Ideologies Are Key to Fighting Campus Sexual Assault

Jamie Utt

In the following viewpoint, Jamie Utt argues that feminism and feminist ideologies are important to overcoming the campus sexual assault problem. He contends that embracing feminism is the best way to change the culture that surrounds and enables college sexual violence. He details what can be done to take a stand against campus sexual assault from a feminist perspective. Utt is a Minnesota-based diversity and inclusion consultant and sexual violence prevention educator as well as a writer for Everyday Feminism.

As you read, consider the following questions:

1. According to Utt, how should individuals change the way they talk about sexual violence?

2. What does Utt say can be done to make college parties safer for all students?

3. According to Utt, why is Amherst College an important example for anti–sexual assault activists?

On every single college campus in the United States, there is a powerful, committed group of feminists and feminist allies who are working to prevent sexual violence and respond to the needs of survivors.

These incredible coalitions of students, professors, staff, administrators, and wider community members are working every single day to ensure that survivors have the support they need while working to prevent further sexual assaults.

Too often, though, they are working against institutions and campus environments that shame survivors, protect perpetrators, and reinforce the rape culture that is endemic in our society.

The Grim Reality and What Can Be Done to Change It

The grim reality is that at least 1 in 4 college women are survivors of sexual violence, and our institutions are not doing enough to stem this terrible tide.

It is time that more of us join these committed activists in transforming the culture and climate of our college and university campuses.

Whether you're a parent, a student, an alumni, or simply a concerned community member, here are a few ways that you can help:

1. Change How We Talk About Sexual Violence.

The messages that are sent to women and men about sexual violence on college campuses tend to be misguided at best and downright dangerous at worst.

Whether the message is delivered formally through a new student orientation program or through norms and mores, the traditional wisdom for sexual violence prevention on college campuses can often be boiled down to: *"Ladies, be careful so you don't get raped."*

Whether we tell women to go out in groups, watch their drinks, or never walk across campus alone at night, the conversation is the same—the responsibility for preventing sexual violence is on women.

But considering that the vast majority of rapes are committed by men, we can't afford to leave men out of the conversation!

To place the responsibility for sexual violence prevention on women not only completely ignores those who perpetrate the majority of sexual assaults, but it lends itself to victim blaming.

"You shouldn't have been dressed that way." "You shouldn't have gone out alone." "You shouldn't have been drinking."

Thus, in both our informal conversations and as we look to change how our institutions address sexual violence, we must shift the conversation to ones of positive sexuality, enthusiastic consent, healthy masculinity, and support for survivors.

First, if sex and sexuality are talked about openly and honestly, we can begin to have more accountable conversations regarding positive sexuality.

We can introduce the ideas behind and methods for realizing enthusiastic consent. We can encourage healthier relationships and healthier sexuality in all their forms. So that people of all genders understand what healthy and consensual sexual relationships can and should look like.

Secondly, we must also end the culture of male sexual entitlement, disrespect, catcalling, and objectification that protects perpetrators of sexual violence.

Men, women have been trying to tell us these things for ages. It's time for us to be the leaders in ending sexual violence. We, as men, need to work with other men to change how we talk about and practice sex.

Third, we need to change how we talk about sexual violence so that it reflects reality and not myths about rape.

A good place to start is changing where we place the onus for prevention. The only person responsible for a sexual assault is the perpetrator. Plain and simple. From there, we can do a better job of supporting those who experience sexual assault.

Finally, we have to make sure that our conversations don't accidentally silence survivors who don't fit our understanding of "normal." Any person of any gender or any sexual orientation can experience sexual violence. 50% of transgender people experience sexual violence and approximately 8% of all men (by conservative estimates) are raped by a former partner.

Often, conversations around rape focus solely on straight relationships, but lesbian, gay, and bisexual people commonly experience sexual violence, too. Further, 1 in 10 survivors of sexual violence are men, and we need to have resources that support male survivors.

Lastly, we need to expand the conversation around sexual violence beyond rape (forced sexual intercourse, including vaginal, anal, or oral penetration) to other types of unwanted sexual contact and coercive sexual activity (including forced kissing, groping, forced hand jobs, nonconsensual kissing, etc.).

Otherwise, those who experience sexual violence that they would not call rape may feel like their experience is not legitimate or worthy of attention. But they often still experience trauma like rape survivors because it was still not consensual.

In short, we can make our conversations more inclusive, and we can push to make our campus programming more inclusive.

Alcohol and Sexual Violence

2. Transform Party Culture.

A tremendous number of sexual assaults take place during or after college parties. Does this mean that parties are evil? Obviously no, but it does beg certain questions about how we can make our parties more sex positive and preventative of sexual violence.

4 in 5 college students drink, and about half of college drinkers engage in heavy binge drinking while attending college parties. While alcohol surely doesn't cause sexual violence, alcohol consumption is a common factor that facilitates sexual violence.

According to one study, 74% of people who have committed sexual violence were under the influence of alcohol when they did it, and 55% of survivors were under the influence of alcohol when they were assaulted.

Now, we must be careful in discussing the link between alcohol and violence because we are not implying that anyone who drinks somehow brings sexual violence on themselves.

But let's be real—people who set out to commit rape use alcohol to incapacitate their victims in a strong majority of their assaults.

So what are we to do? Well, the solution is definitely not to call for some kind of new temperance movement or simply to tell women to watch their drinks.

Instead, researchers A. Ayres Boswell and Joan Z. Spade identify characteristics of parties that are higher risk for sexual violence in contrast with parties that are of lower risk for sexual violence.

For example, parties where drinking is more casual, with less alcohol consumed over more time, are linked to fewer assaults than parties where binge drinking is the norm.

Parties where there is a tolerance for jokes, conversations, and behavior that degrades women are of higher risk, but parties where there is a lot of conversation and respectful socialization between men and women are linked to lower rates of sexual violence.

In short, if we make our parties more sex positive and respectful while encouraging responsible drinking, we can throw parties that are not only tons of fun but that are preventative of sexual violence.

Survivors Need Encouragement

3. Believe and Support Survivors.

One of the many roles of sexual assault survivors' advocates is to listen to survivors, believe and affirm their story, and help them understand what they need to heal.

Rarely, though, do survivors choose to publicly discuss their experience or press charges, either legally or within the disciplinary system of their college or university.

And why would survivors want to publicly acknowledge their assault? Often when survivors do, they are treated both socially and institutionally as if they are lying or as if they somehow did something to deserve the assault.

Unfortunately, whether they are seeking legal justice or a school disciplinary response, pressing any sort of charges is likely to be hell for the survivor. They will have to tell their story over and over, and they will be put on public trial, being accused of dressing or acting in a way that invited assault.

But we don't need to stand for this. One of the most sustaining aspects of rape culture is its ability to silence survivors for fear of this type of treatment. In order to change this, we have to speak out in support of survivors, believe and affirm survivors when they share their stories, and hold people accountable to their words and actions.

When someone says something that shames or blames survivors, more of us must speak out. When someone acts to objectify or disrespect women, more of us must speak out.

Men must transform our relationships with other men to be ones of positive masculinity and healthy sexuality. People of all genders must work in coalition to end the silencing and to expose rape culture everywhere it exists.

This seems simple, but we need more people to join us in this struggle.

Prevention Programs to Curb Sexual Violence on Campus Are Essential

4. Focus on Prevention, Too.

Most institutions do have some sort of sexual violence response protocol: counseling services, advertised hotlines, health services, peer advocates, and disciplinary actions (though it rarely gets that far).

Setting aside the varying effectiveness of these response protocols, these services are vitally important for supporting survivors.

The problem, though, is that they are limited. They quite necessarily focus on responding to sexual violence once it has happened. While this is important, it's not enough.

We must continue to demand that our institutions invest resources and attention toward prevention.

In my work, I often reach out to colleges and universities in hopes of connecting with those on campus responsible for sexual violence prevention. Far too often, though, I am told, "We don't really have someone responsible for that. Do you mean counseling services?"

With endless research-driven approaches, resources, programs, and trainings that focus on primary prevention, there are countless viable ways that we can be engaging in prevention work on our campuses.

But this takes a financial and comprehensive commitment from the institution. We all know how hard it is to ensure new financial commitments (no matter how small) in the era of belt tightening and budget cuts.

But if enough members of our communities are demanding it, our administrators will have no choice but to listen.

Institutions Need to Be Responsible and Accountable

5. Demand More Supportive and Responsive Institutions.

The other side of ending rape culture involves addressing how our institutions respond to sexual violence.

In 2012, Amherst College was rocked by a sexual assault scandal. Angie Epifano was raped by another student while attending Amherst. When she sought help through the college's counseling services and her dean, she was told to simply get over it and move on.

The college, a highly respected liberal arts institution, literally did every single thing wrong that it could possibly do, and when Epifano shared her story publicly, numerous other survivors came forward with similar stories.

It's sad that it took a survivor publicly sharing her story like this in order to force an institution to change. But if there's any silver lining in this terrible tale, it's that Amherst's president, Biddy Martin, didn't shy away from responsibility.

She acknowledged that Amherst had failed its students, particularly its student survivors, and she vowed to make the college a national leader in sexual assault prevention and response.

Since that time, the institution has committed itself to improving counseling services, expanding prevention efforts, and listening to feminist activists who have been calling for changes for decades.

Amherst is simultaneously an example of the terrible ways in which academic institutions often respond to sexual violence on their campuses AND of the powerful changes that can take place in how institutions respond to this violence.

Moving forward, we must ensure that it doesn't take more trauma like that which Epifano experienced to force our institutions to change.

Change Is Possible

Ask any committed activist: Transforming our institutions will not be easy.

It will take coalitions of people of every race, religion, ability, gender, sexual orientation, citizenship status, and level of wealth.

It will take coalitions of students, professors, parents, staff, administrators, and community members.

But the beauty is that we already have powerful leaders and models from every one of these areas of our communities.

We have activists and advocates and allies who need our help. Our institutions can only marginalize our voices if we're fractured and disparate.

We must rise.

> "If the feminist movement is not elastic enough for self-awareness, self-evaluation and self-critique with a spectrum of differing viewpoints, then it's not the strong movement it purports to be."

Feminists Are Failing to Address Campus Sexual Assault Effectively

Brett Milam

In the following viewpoint, Brett Milam argues that feminists' current approach to the campus sexual assault problem is misguided and only making the situation worse. He contends that white feminists are focusing on the campus sexual assault problem too aggressively and are excluding key minority voices from their dialogue. Further, he reports that the feminist approach to campus sexual assault is reinforcing the gender stereotypes that have helped create the problem in the first place. At the time of writing, Milam was a student at Miami University of Ohio and a staff member of the Miami Student *newspaper.*

As you read, consider the following questions:

1. According to Milam, why is it wrong for feminists to brand the college sexual assault problem an epidemic?

2. How has feminism's shaping of sexual encounters hurt women, according to the viewpoint?

3. According to Milam, in what way does feminism need to change?

Feminists, despite having the best of intentions, have gone too far in their efforts to respond to sexual assaults on college campuses.

Feminism and Rape Culture

I consider myself a feminist because I believe there are systemic issues at play in our patriarchal society, most salient in rape culture.

Rape culture is evidenced by how much rape goes unreported (68 percent, according to RAINN [Rape, Abuse, and Incest National Network]), with how many college campuses cover up rape for a variety of reasons (94 institutions have pending Title IX investigations from the Department of Education, according to *ThinkProgress*) and the enormous rape kit backlog (400,000 according to the Daily Beast).

Even with all of that in consideration, feminists are missing the mark by focusing so much on the "college rape crisis." In other words, white, middle-class feminists are dominating the conversation and because of that, the focus is on college rape.

The Facts

As point of fact, women who don't go to college are more likely to be raped than women who do.

Callie Marie Rennison, writing in the *New York Times*, talks about a study she coauthored with Lynn Addington where they examined the Department of Justice's National Crime Victimization Survey data from 1995 to 2011.

"We found that the estimated rate of sexual assault and rape of female college students, ages 18 to 24, was 6.1 per 1,000 students. This is nothing to be proud of, but it is significantly lower than the rate experienced by women that age who don't attend college—eight per 1,000," she said.

Disadvantaged women—that is, women with little money, few resources and little education—are the ones who "bear the brunt of the harshest realities, including sexual violence," she said.

Who Leads the Feminist Dialogue on Sexual Assault?

Rennison cautions against the obvious: Nobody is saying ignore sexual violence against the wealthy and the educated, but it's important to be cognizant of which voices (white, middle class) are dominating the narrative. To elaborate on the race point, black women are more likely to be raped (18.8 percent compared to 17.7 percent for white women), but black voices and the intersectionality of feminism and race are hardly cornerstones of modern, mainstream feminism.

Or what about the patronizing white savior complex applied to Muslim women wearing the hijab [traditional covering for the hair and neck]? Myriam Francois-Cerrah gave a talk to the Oxford Union [Society] and spoke about how dominant white culture subjugates people of color to a second-class status and, specifically, women.

"When it comes to alternative conceptions of feminism, the feminist movement has been doggedly resistant to including alternative voices," she said.

These critiques of white feminism, which means mainstream feminism, are important to be cognizant of and to work to change. It's also important to temper our use of "epidemic" when applying it to college rape when the statistics just don't bare it out.

The Problem with Modern Feminism

The feminists of today have come to embody everything that they purport to be against. That is to say, they more closely resemble a conservative movement in the mainstream rather than a progressive one. Perhaps most ironically, their rather Puritan conception of sexual encounters has reduced a woman's agency and autonomy, which then has the effect of leaning too heavily on men.

One relevant case study can be found within the folds of this newspaper. University editor Emily Tate wrote an opinion piece ("Males May Find Themselves at the Mercy of Women in Alcohol-Related Hookups"), which was much maligned.

Most of the ire I saw was directed at her statistics and the conclusions she drew from them. First, her statistic that one in 12 men has admitted to the legal understanding of rape (despite not labeling themselves rapists) is accurate. On the other hand, the statistic that one in four women will be the victim of sexual assault is now widely disputed.

New York Sen. Kirsten Gillibrand, someone pushing legislation to fine schools for underreporting rape, even took the stat off her website.

Secondly, the conclusion Ms. Tate drew from the statistics does not at all seem controversial.

"These don't add up. So, perhaps we should consider that a female's definition of sexual assault does not always align with a male's. That, of course, is the issue," she said.

Is it not the issue that men and women understand sexual encounters differently, thus leading to murky territory over consent?

Activism and Sexual Violence

We learned about high-profile rape cases at Vanderbilt [University] and the University of Montana, about "trigger warnings" and "safe spaces," and *Rolling Stone*'s misreported story of a phantom University of Virginia gang rape. It's hard to talk about higher education at all these days without mentioning the activism around sexual assault and women's issues. . . .

Why, when there is so much serious work to be done, does this new generation of feminists only look inward instead of out at the big world? . . .

I hope the wounded women at our colleges and universities find a way to heal themselves and then get to work in the places they're needed most. I hope they take all the passion, anger and energy they've applied to making college administrators figure out when yes means yes and no means no, and harness it to address problems far beyond their own.

Meghan Daum,
"Time for Young Feminists to Look Beyond the Mattress and Campus Rape," Los Angeles Times, *May 26, 2015.*

The Meaning of Sexual Assault

Now, about that definition of sexual assault. In a letter to the editor ("It's On Us: Affirmative Consent Standard Reduces Ambiguity"), the authors believe their definition eliminates ambiguity.

"Any person who initiates sexual activity is responsible for obtaining a verbal 'yes' from the other person throughout the sexual encounter," the authors said.

I find that deeply troubling. It goes to my point of applying a conservative, Puritanical concept of sex on men and women. Obtaining a verbal "yes" throughout negates potential nonverbal cues and takes away the sexy from the sex. They argue it erases ambiguity, but what does "throughout" look like in practice? It's also important to note that rape occurring in this ambiguous space of drunk consent is not all that common. Amanda Marcotte for *Slate* noted as much.

"The high rates of campus sexual assault are due mostly to a small percentage of men who assault multiple women," she said.

As for the crux of Ms. Tate's article, that the adjudication process has gone too far in hurting men in the name of protecting women, she's also right in that critique.

Sending the Wrong Message

Another *Slate* writer, Emily Yoffe, offers a blistering review of the new documentary *The Hunting Ground*, which probes sexual assaults on college campuses, when she says moral panic has "clouded our ability to rationally assess the problem." Yoffe further acknowledges that it's good to teach a generation of young men that it's never okay to pressure women into sex.

But, "We are also teaching a generation of young women that they are malleable, weak, 'overwhelmed' and helpless in the face of male persuasion," she said.

Indeed. As Ms. Tate noted, drunk men are responsible for their actions, whatever they may be, but the process says a drunk woman is not. She's just a helpless victim. This goes against everything I understand feminism to be in terms of empowering women and giving them their due agency. Whether a woman consented or not is being turned over to college bureaucracies to adjudicate, which, again, diminishes a woman's control over her own body.

Reevaluating Feminism

Feminists ought to be able to handle necessary self-examination, to see how their solutions are doing and if they've gone too far. It is my belief that they have.

Worse yet, much like a conservative strain of thought, feminists of today want to censor differing viewpoints. Many of Ms. Tate's detractors wished the *Miami Student* had never published her piece. Why?

If the feminist movement is not elastic enough for self-awareness, self-evaluation and self-critique with a spectrum of differing viewpoints, then it's not the strong movement it purports to be.

Periodical and Internet Sources Bibliography

The following articles have been selected to supplement the diverse views presented in this chapter.

| Robert Carle | "How Affirmative Consent Laws Criminalize Everyone," *Federalist*, March 30, 2015. |

| Jonathan Chait | "Feminists Criticizing Campus Sexual Assault Rules," *New York*, February 24, 2015. |

| Mona Charen | "Feminist Lies About Sexual Assault," *National Review Online*, October 3, 2014. |

| Jordan Chariton | "After *Rolling Stone* Debacle, Will Sexual Assault Survivors Trust the Media?," The Wrap, April 10, 2015. |

| Tara Culp-Ressler | "The College Sexual Assault Crisis Turns a Corner," *ThinkProgress*, April 29, 2014. |

| Conor Friedersdorf | "An Appalling Case for Affirmative-Consent Laws," *Atlantic*, October 16, 2014. |

| Samantha Harris | "One in Five? The White House's Questionable Sexual Assault Data," *Forbes*, May 7, 2014. |

| Amanda Hess | "'No Means No' Isn't Enough. We Need Affirmative Consent Laws to Curb Sexual Assault," *Slate*, June 16, 2014. |

| Jenny Kutner | "Yes to 'Yes Means Yes': California's Affirmative Consent Law Is the First Step to Eradicating Campus Sexual Assault," *Salon*, September 29, 2014. |

| Naomi Shatz | "Feminists, We Are Not Winning the War on Campus Sexual Assault," *Huffington Post*, October 29, 2014. |

For Further Discussion

Chapter 1

1. Angela Carone and Blaize Stewart take opposite positions on the question of whether fraternities should be held responsible for the campus sexual assault problem. With which author do you agree more, and why? Explain your answer.

2. Barbara J. King argues that the root cause of the campus sexual assault problem is the existence of a "rape culture" in America. Do you believe that "rape culture" exists? Why, or why not?

3. Antonia Abbey asserts that alcohol is the primary factor in campus sexual assaults, while Daniel Luzer contends that it is not. In your opinion, which author does a better job of presenting his or her argument? Why? Who would you say is right? Explain your reasoning.

Chapter 2

1. Judith Shulevitz argues that the way most colleges adjudicate campus sexual assault cases is unfair to the accused. Do you agree with her argument, or do you think the current system is fair to both parties? Explain your answer.

2. David M. Rubin contends that campus sexual assault cases should be handled by the police, while Caroline Heldman and Baillee Brown say colleges should continue to be responsible for adjudicating such cases. Who do you think should adjudicate campus sexual assault cases, and why? Cite text from the viewpoints to support your answer.

3. Kinjo Kiema asserts that students found guilty of sexual assault should be subject to mandatory expulsion. Do you think this would be an appropriate response? Why, or why not?

Chapter 3

1. Adam B. Summers and Lauren Barbato take opposite sides in the argument over whether allowing students to carry guns on campus would help to alleviate the campus sexual assault problem. With which argument do you agree more? Explain your answer.

2. Marissa Miller and Tara Culp-Ressler offer differing opinions on whether sexual assault prevention smartphone apps would help to address the campus sexual assault problem. Do you think such apps would make a significant impact on the problem? Why, or why not?

3. Sarah Robertson believes that allowing sororities to hold their own parties would be a good way to address the campus sexual assault problem. In your opinion, would sorority parties help to reduce campus sexual violence? Why, or why not?

Chapter 4

1. Melanie Boyd and Joseph Fischel argue that affirmative consent laws will help correct the campus sexual assault problem, while Masha Gershman asserts the laws will only make the situation worse. What impact do you think affirmative consent laws will have on sexual assaults on campuses? Explain your answer.

2. Jamie Stiehm and John Stossel express very different opinions on how media outlets report on the issue of college sexual assault. Do you think news media are doing a good job covering sexual assaults on campuses? Why, or why not?

3. Brett Milam argues that feminists are off base when it comes to the campus sexual assault problem. How do you think Jamie Utt would respond to Milam's argument? Explain.

Organizations to Contact

The editors have compiled the following list of organizations concerned with the issues debated in this book. The descriptions are derived from materials provided by the organizations. All have publications or information available for interested readers. The list was compiled on the date of publication of the present volume; the information provided here may change. Be aware that many organizations take several weeks or longer to respond to inquiries, so allow as much time as possible.

American Association of University Women (AAUW)
1111 Sixteenth Street NW, Washington, DC 20036
(202) 785-7700
e-mail: connect@aauw.org
website: www.aauw.org

Since its founding in 1881, the American Association of University Women (AAUW) has worked to promote equity for women in education and employment. Most of the AAUW's efforts aim to ensure that women across the nation have an equal opportunity to reap the benefits of quality education and fair compensation in the workplace. The organization also takes a strong stand against campus sexual assault, providing survivors and activists with a wide array of information and tools to use in the fight against the epidemic of sexual violence at American colleges. The AAUW publishes a range of informative newsletters, position papers, brochures, and more, including the periodical *AAUW Outlook* magazine.

Campus Outreach Services (COS)
PO Box 332, Wayne, PA 19087
(866) 966-9901
e-mail: Inspire@CampusOutreachServices.com
website: http://campusoutreachservices.com

Campus Outreach Services (COS) is a for-profit organization that provides wellness and safety services to more than three thousand colleges, high schools, military bases, youth groups, and corporations around the world. COS was founded in 1994 by Katie Koestner, who at only age eighteen spoke out nationally about her own victimization by a fellow college student. As the first survivor of date rape to tell her story publically to a national audience, Koestner broke a long silence. COS areas of expertise include sexual violence, digital citizenship, substance use, diversity, sexual harassment, bullying, healthy relationships, body image, mental health, and related risk issues. The COS website provides descriptions of the many programs and services the organization offers.

Institute on Violence, Abuse and Trauma (IVAT)

10065 Old Grove Road, San Diego, CA   92131
(858) 527-1860 • fax: (858) 527-1743
e-mail: ivat@alliant.edu
website: www.ivatcenters.org

The Institute on Violence, Abuse and Trauma (IVAT), formed through a merger of the Family Violence and Sexual Assault Institute (FVSAI) and Alliant International University, is a leading international resource, research, and training center that provides information and services related to all areas of violence, abuse, and trauma. Through its various programs, which focus on sexual assault, workplace violence, youth and school violence, traumatic stress, and violence prevention, IVAT seeks to discourage violence and elevate the quality of life for people across the country and around the world.

National Alliance to End Sexual Violence (NAESV)

1130 Connecticut Avenue NW, Suite 300
Washington, DC   20036
e-mail: info@endsexualviolence.org
website: http://endsexualviolence.org

The National Alliance to End Sexual Violence (NAESV) is a nonprofit organization that works in support of the advancement of public policy on behalf of state coalitions, individuals, and other entities seeking to bring an end to sexual violence. NAESV advocates on behalf of sexual assault victims of all ages and genders and maintains a comprehensive grass-roots communication network designed to help advance national policy related to sexual violence and victims' needs; fund rape crisis programs and sexual assault coalitions; and provide governments, businesses, and nonprofit organizations with the information and expertise necessary to effectively address all forms of sexual violence.

National Center on Domestic and Sexual Violence (NCDSV)
(800) 799-7233
e-mail: dtucker@ncdsv.org
website: www.ncdsv.org

The National Center on Domestic and Sexual Violence (NCDSV) is a nonprofit organization whose mission is to encourage and create collaboration among professionals working to end violence against women. NCDSV trains professionals who work with victims and perpetrators of violent crimes, including professionals in law enforcement and criminal justice, health care, counseling and social work, and advocacy and service provision. The NCDSV website provides links to publications, articles, and reports related to many topics, including sexual violence on campus.

Office on Violence Against Women (OVW)
145 N Street NE, Suite 10W.121, Washington, DC   20530
(202) 307-6026 • fax: (202) 305-2589
e-mail: ovw.info@usdoj.gov
website: www.justice.gov/ovw

The Office on Violence Against Women (OVW), a component of the US Department of Justice, works to reduce all forms of violence against women and provide the survivors of such violence with the justice and support they deserve. The OVW fulfills its commitment to fighting sexual assault and supporting survivors primarily through discretionary grant programs, providing pivotal funding for state, local, and tribal governments; nonprofit and community-based organizations; and other entities that actively seek to develop better responses to violence against women. Through its grant programs, the OVW ensures that victims of sexual assault have access to the support they need to cope with the trauma they have endured and that communities have the resources necessary to bring offenders to justice.

One Student

303 Main Street #1414, Safety Harbor, FL 34695
(813) 789-1256
e-mail: info@onestudent.org
website: http://onestudent.org

One Student is a nonprofit organization that provides cutting-edge programs, resources, and opportunities that engage students to create social change to reduce sexual violence. It encourages students to talk about sexual assault and healthy sexuality within their communities; increases knowledge about sexual violence through programming, outreach, and online resources; educates students on immediate actions they can take as bystanders in potential or actual situations of sexual violence; engages stakeholders on college campuses to lead their communities toward zero tolerance for sexual violence; and provides support for parents of teenage and adult victims of sexual assault.

People Against Rape (PAR)

PO Box 1723, Charleston, SC 29402
(843) 577-9882
e-mail: ExecDirector@PeopleAgainstRape.org
website: www.peopleagainstrape.org

People Against Rape (PAR) primarily seeks to prevent teens and kids from becoming the victims of sexual assault and rape by offering instruction in self-defense. In addition, PAR also works to promote self-esteem and motivation among high school and college students through an array of specialized educational programs. As part of its commitment to fighting sexual assault, PAR produces and distributes a number of publications, including "Defend: Preventing Date Rape and Other Sexual Assaults" and "Sexual Assault: How to Defend Yourself."

Prevention Institute

221 Oak Street, Oakland, CA 94607
(510) 444-7738 • fax: (510) 663-1280
e-mail: prevent@preventioninstitute.org
website: www.preventioninstitute.org

The Prevention Institute takes a broad approach to supporting violence prevention by facilitating projects, researching and reporting on violence in all its forms, evaluating violence prevention strategies, and conducting training seminars. Through its local, state, and national training efforts, the Prevention Institute has established itself as a widely recognized leader in the prevention of youth violence, rape and sexual assault, child abuse, hate-related violence, domestic violence, and more.

Rape, Abuse, and Incest National Network (RAINN)

1220 L Street NW, Suite 505, Washington, DC 20005
(202) 544-1034
e-mail: info@rainn.org
website: www.rainn.org

The Rape, Abuse, and Incest National Network (RAINN) operates a national hotline for sexual assault victims. RAINN's hotline provides survivors nationwide with free, confidential counseling and support services around the clock. Among many other things, RAINN is deeply dedicated to the issue of college sexual assault and campus safety. As part of its efforts, RAINN coordinates RAINN Day on American college campuses every September. On RAINN Day, organizers educate thousands of students about sexual assault through various special events and by handing out informative wallet cards that feature helpful information about sexual violence.

Students Active for Ending Rape (SAFER)

32 Broadway #1101, New York, NY 10004
(347) 465-7233
website: http://safercampus.org

A campus organization founded by students at Columbia University in 2000, Students Active for Ending Rape (SAFER) strives to combat college sexual assault by empowering students and ensuring that they have the information and support they need to make a difference. SAFER provides training materials, workshops, mentoring, and an online resource library—all of which are designed to help students get organized and take action against the growing problem of campus sexual assault. The organization also has compiled a Campus Sexual Assault Policies Database, which allows users to easily explore and learn about how college campuses across the country deal with sexual assault and what they could and should be doing better.

Bibliography of Books

Arthur S. Chancellor

Investigating Sexual Assault Cases. Burlington, MA: Jones & Bartlett, 2014.

William D. Cohan

The Price of Silence: The Duke Lacrosse Scandal, the Power of the Elite, and the Corruption of Our Great Universities. New York: Scribner, 2014.

Christopher J. Correia, James G. Murphy, and Nancy P. Barnett

College Student Alcohol Abuse: A Guide to Assessment, Intervention, and Prevention. New York: John Wiley & Sons, 2012.

John Davis

How to Avoid False Accusations of Rape: Self Defense in the Feminist State. Cranbury, NJ: Old Town Publishing, 2015.

Alan DeSantis

Inside Greek U.: Fraternities, Sororities, and the Pursuit of Pleasure, Power, and Prestige. Lexington: University Press of Kentucky, 2007.

Danielle Dirks

Confronting Campus Rape: Legal Landscapes, New Media, and Networked Activism. New York: Routledge, 2015.

George W. Dowdall

College Drinking: Reframing a Social Problem/Changing the Culture. Sterling, VA: Stylus Publishing, 2012.

Bonnie S. Fisher and John J. Sloan III, eds. *Campus Crime: Legal, Social, and Policy Perspectives.* Springfield, IL: Charles C. Thomas, 2013.

R. Barri Flowers *College Crime: A Statistical Study of Offenses on American Campuses.* Jefferson, NC: McFarland, 2009.

Jerlando F.L. Jackson and Melvin Cleveland Terrell, eds. *Creating and Maintaining Safe College Campuses: A Sourcebook for Enhancing and Evaluating Safety Programs.* Sterling, VA: Stylus Publishing, 2007.

Jon Krakauer *Missoula: Rape and the Justice System in a College Town.* New York: Doubleday, 2015.

Michele A. Paludi and Florence L. Denmark *Victims of Sexual Assault and Abuse: Incidence and Psychological Dimensions.* Santa Barbara, CA: Praeger, 2010.

Nick T. Pappas *The Dark Side of Sports: Exposing the Sexual Culture of Collegiate and Professional Athletes.* Indianapolis, IN: Meyer & Meyer Sport, 2012.

Peggy Reeves Sanday *Fraternity Gang Rape: Sex, Brotherhood, and Privilege on Campus.* New York: New York University Press, 2007.

Liz Seccuro *Crash into Me: A Survivor's Search for Justice.* New York: Bloomsbury USA, 2011.

Michael L. Seigel *Race to Injustice: Lessons Learned from the Duke Lacrosse Rape Case.* Durham, NC: Carolina Academic Press, 2009.

John J. Sloan III and Bonnie S. Fisher *The Dark Side of the Ivory Tower: Campus Crime as a Social Problem.* New York: Cambridge University Press, 2010.

Brian Van Brunt *Ending Campus Violence: New Approaches to Prevention.* New York: Routledge, 2012.

Thomas Vander Ven *Getting Wasted: Why College Students Drink Too Much and Party So Hard.* New York: New York University Press, 2011.

Michael P. Watts, ed. *Sexual Violence on Campus: Overview, Issues and Actions.* Hauppauge, NY: Nova Science Publishers, 2015.

Karen G. Weiss *Party School: Crime, Campus, and Community.* Lebanon, NH: University Press of New England, 2013.

Leighton Whitaker and Jeffrey Pollard *Campus Violence: Kinds, Causes, and Cures.* New York: Routledge, 2014.

Sara Carrigan Wooten and Roland W. Mitchell, eds. *The Crisis of Campus Sexual Violence: Critical Perspectives on Prevention and Response.* New York: Routledge, 2015.

Index